muddy roads

blue
skies

My Journey to the Foreign Service,
From the Rural South to Tanzania and Beyond

VELLA MBENNA

MUDDY ROADS PRESS
AMELIA ISLAND, FLORIDA

Muddy Roads Press
P.O. Box 15065
Amelia Island, FL 32034
vellagmbenna@gmail.com

Editor and Project Manager: Marla Markman, www.marlamarkman.com
Cover and Interior Design: GKS Creative, www.gkscreative.com

Disclaimers: Names contained in this book have been changed to protect their identities, and the views expressed in this book are those of the author and not necessarily of the U.S. government.

Publisher's Cataloging-in-Publication Data

Names: Mbenna, Vella, author.
Title: Muddy roads blue skies : my journey to the Foreign Service, from the rural South to Tanzania and beyond / Vella Mbenna.
Description: Amelia Island, FL: Muddy Roads Press, 2019.
Identifiers: LCCN 2018911257 | ISBN 978-1-7327918-0-0 (pbk.) | 978-1-7327918-1-7 (ebook)
Subjects: LCSH Mbenna, Vella. | United States. Foreign Service--Officials and employees--Biography. | Diplomats--United States--Biography. | Diplomatic and consular service, American--History--20th century. | United States--Foreign relations--20th century. | BISAC BIOGRAPHY & AUTOBIOGRAPHY / Personal Memoirs |
Classification: LCC E840.8.M255 2019 | DDC 327.730092--dc23

978-1-7327918-0-0 (Softcover)
978-1-7327918-1-7 (eReaders)

Library of Congress Control Number: 2018911257

Printed in the United States of America

Dedication

I dedicate this book to my husband, Shaka; our son, Andrew; our three grandchildren, Keegan, Ian, and Anah; and my parents— Eugene and Martha Rae.

Shaka, I love and thank you from the bottom of my heart for what you have done to and for me—you opened my eyes to a new way of thinking and living when I thought I was already on top of the world. Keep pushing me to the next level. I love it and I love you!

Andrew, God gave me the right bundle of joy to be there for me when there would be no one else around who cared for so many years and so far away from home. I followed my passion with God, great values, and you by my side; now you follow yours with the same and knowing I will be right by your side, as always. Son, understanding me will enable you to understand yourself and appreciate love, career, family, friends, religion, etc. This project would still be a thought if you had not encouraged me to make it a reality—it is my legacy to you.

Keegan, Ian, and Anah, when I thought retirement was the end and I would sit by the seaside fading away, your three heart- beats put me on a path of grandmotherhood I never imagined and given me yet another reason for completing this project as a legacy. I love you, love you, love you!

Momma and Daddy (if you hear me from heaven), all I can say is, "Thank you for how you raised me and for always believing in and loving me, especially as I screwed up my life over and over again until I got it right." What you did for me placed me on a path to be able to leave this legacy behind for the family because it not only tells my story, but our family story, in part.

Acknowledgments

I would like to take this opportunity to thank God and several very special people who have encouraged, advised, assisted, or supported me in this book project.

The initial seed to write this book came from my dear son, Andrew, who encouraged me many years ago to write a book about my life and include some of the things I experienced in my amazing career in the Foreign Service.

My dear husband, Shaka, played the most supportive role in this journey, keeping me focused and allowing nothing to obstruct me from completing this project. Thank you so much.

A very special and heartfelt thank you goes to Heidi King, the wind beneath my wings on this project. Thanks to her friendship and professional expertise as a writer, she got to know me and was able to take a myriad of my tiny stories and condense them into a legible manuscript.

Words cannot express my gratitude to my project manager and editor, Marla Markman, for her professional advice and assistance in polishing this manuscript and making it ready for the press.

Table of Contents

Discovery

*Beyond the small town, it's huge, complex, distant,
mysterious, and frightening, but it can be interesting,
beautiful, accessible, friendly, and unforgettable if you dare
to take the challenge!*

There was a time in my life when I was going nowhere fast. In a span of three years after college, a failed marriage left me broke, humiliated, without a career, and with a baby to care for on my own. I had no choice but to tuck my tail between my legs and head back to my parents' home in the Holmestown community of Midway, Georgia. I had spent my whole life planning to get out, and I did—or so I thought. But now I had returned, defeated and ashamed. I spiraled into depression, unable to see past the haze that clouded every day much less imagine a life out there, somewhere far away from that red-dirt, dead-end muddy road on which my parents' house was perched.

And yet, far away is where I found myself on August 7, 1998. It was a crisp and clear Tanzanian morning. Sipping Chai Bora tea, I smiled, savoring the view and smell of the beautiful Indian Ocean sprawled in front of my house. It was what I had awakened to and enjoyed every morning before going to work for the past two years while assigned to the US Embassy in Dar es Salaam, Tanzania, in East Africa. One week before departing Tanzania for my next country of assignment, nothing had changed—everything was as perfect as when I had arrived. The country was not "the armpit of Africa," as a colleague had described it to me while in training. If anything, it was a crown jewel.

The evening before, friends and colleagues from the embassy stopped by my home to sort through things that I had no desire to take with me to my next assignment: a television, one suitcase, some jewelry, a few clocks, clothing and shoes, kitchen utensils and pots, mismatched dishes, food, cleaning products, knick-knacks—you name it, it was for the taking. Watching them carry away the last of my things felt like shedding skin. A new me, vibrant and fresh, waited impatiently underneath. In one week, I would be departing for my next post of assignment in Beirut, Lebanon, the "Paris of the Middle East," as it was once called.

Historically, Beirut had been a romantic, highly sought-after post of assignment for diplomats. However, since the 1983 bombing of the marine barracks in Beirut that claimed 299 lives, 241 of which were Americans, it had fallen out of favor. Still, I was happy to have been assigned there—it was my number-one choice. Furthermore, it would be my first time as an official Information Programs Officer (IPO), running my own shop in charge of information technology (IT) and communications for the embassy, and I desperately wanted to prove myself in a difficult and dangerous post.

It sounds like a death wish or a career-ender, doesn't it?

Back then, the more dangerous and challenging the assignments were, the more I wanted them. Although overwhelming at times, they gave me the rush I craved. *I am in the Foreign Service, and*

Prologue: Discovery

it's my duty to go to these challenging and dangerous places to serve my country (and have fun, too). That was my attitude throughout my career.

Security would be tight in Beirut, which meant living in close quarters on a secure compound. Space would be scarce, hence the need to take only the essentials. One large suitcase and a few small boxes of household effects were all I gave the movers earlier in the week to ship from Dar es Salaam to Beirut.

With my Beirut shipment gone, my remaining household effects packed for storage, and my backpack and carry-on ready to go, I woke up that glorious Tanzanian morning feeling light and unencumbered. Waking up in a near empty, quiet house signaled the start of a rebirth that happens with every new diplomatic assignment. It was one of my favorite things about being in the Foreign Service—a new place, new culture, new challenges, new colleagues, and the luxury of becoming a different person every one to three years. The only constant was the type of work I did. However, I welcomed all the changes. It is true when they say that you become a lifelong learner in the Foreign Service. We are always learning something new—languages, systems, equipment, procedures, cultures, names, combinations, passwords, cooking styles, you name it. So, although I was sad about leaving the beautiful country of Tanzania, where the people and scenery captivated me and my family, there were many more countries I would be assigned to fall in love with in my career. I snapped out of my slumber to mentally and physically prepare for my last Friday in Tanzania.

I dressed in a brown African pants outfit that Friday and threw my chocolate-colored knitted purse I got in Guatemala over my shoulder. The purse sagged with expensive jewelry, including several Tanzanite pieces and my Rolex watch I hardly wore, important personal documents, other valuables I didn't trust to a moving company, and a few remaining small items I would carry in to give to local Tanzanian staff, also known as Foreign Service National (FSN) staff.

Arriving early to the embassy, I parked next to the security guard shack, as I had done each morning for two years, if no one got there before me. There was so much I had to do that day—finalize the sale of my car, complete handover notes for the new Information Management Officer (IMO) who was arriving in two weeks, familiarize the newly arrived Information Management Specialist (IMS) with the operation, and cash a check for the weekend to buy rounds of *nyama choma* (roasted meat I so loved to eat) and Kilimanjaro beers (my favorite) for friends to celebrate my upcoming departure. I passed the security guard shack, and a female Tanzanian guard came out. She and I used to exchange the long Tanzanian greetings every time we saw each other. With her big, sweet smile, she handed me her application for the vacant operator position at my switchboard. I hoped she would get it because she was such a nice young woman who desperately wanted to increase her status from a job where she had to stand all day in the smothering Tanzanian heat alongside male colleagues to one inside the air-conditioned embassy.

Walking slowly to the second floor of the chancery embassy, I distributed small tokens of appreciation from my purse to any FSN staff I met. Tanzanians have beautiful and sincere smiles, so I loved making jokes and giving them reasons to smile. That morning, I was blessed with lots of smiles, as they said *"Asante sana dada,"* which means "Thank you very much, sister." I loved saying *"Karibu sana"* in return: "You are very welcome." My

Swahili had become acceptable after two years of speaking it every chance I got.

Shortly after I entered my office suite, the newly arrived IMS called for me to open the communications center's door for her. She shadowed me as I performed the morning IT and communications checks for functionality. All systems tested operational. Soon after, the IMS went downstairs to complete in-processing with other sections in the embassy.

While the IMS was away, I asked my FSN operator to call the Regional Information Management Center (RIMC) at our embassy in Pretoria, South Africa. I needed to know why they had not confirmed my FSN computer manager's enrollment in the new Windows class. The next session of the class was not going to start anytime in the near future. As the embassy's computer manager, he needed to take the Windows class sooner than later.

Knowing the connection to Pretoria would take five minutes or so, I grabbed my checkbook and dashed out the suite door to cash a check in the administrative section of the unclassified portion of the embassy, only to do an about-face when I heard my phone ring. Yes, it was the call to Embassy Pretoria, and I had just the person I needed to talk to on the line. I sat down and began talking with her.

Suddenly, a loud *kaboom* punctured the peace of the morning. Still sitting in my chair, I went sailing across the floor before slamming into the racks of communication equipment behind me. The force threw me off the chair and onto the floor. Confused and dazed, I struggled to pull myself up. I saw chaos in the suite. What happened?

My head was throbbing, ears ringing, hands shaking, and knees wobbly. Standing did not provide any more insight into the situation. The security strobe light in the suite flashed bright red while the public announcement system in the building wailed, "EVACUATE THE BUILDING, THIS IS NOT A DRILL! EVACUATE THE BUILDING, THIS IS NOT A DRILL!"

A sane person would have headed for the door and gotten the hell out of there as instructed. Not me. Instead, I dashed to the telegraphic system and sent out a one-sentence service message to our stateside team, informing them that something unknown but bad had occurred at the embassy and they were to close the circuit. Still staggering, I went from one piece of equipment to the next, powering down or switching to a safe mode. In between, I kept calling my operator to patch me through to the RIMC in Pretoria for guidance, but I could not get the operator. I was becoming frustrated, and before it showed, I decided to place the call myself. Guess what? The lines were busy. I tried calling our embassy in Nairobi, Kenya, and could not get through to them either. That was odd but not too alarming because sometimes the lines into countries get busy during the morning hours. So, I called both entities on the high-frequency (HF) radio—still nothing. At that point, I was worried and a bit scared. I gave up trying to find help. It felt as if I was on my own to make needed communication decisions (and safety decisions pertaining to my own life).

After the attempts to reach Pretoria and Nairobi without luck, I peeped beyond my door to see what was happening. I shook. Doors were down or hanging on hinges; the place looked like a hurricane swept through it, merciless.

I retreated to my office suite and closed one of the only doors in sight that was still intact.

I repeated the sanitizing routine again, just to be certain I did not miss anything. I called Pretoria and Nairobi again. Still no response. I used my embassy-issued handheld radio to try reaching the Marines downstairs. No response.

This meant only one thing: the antennas on the embassy roof were down, and I needed to get to my house a mile away to bring the backup networks online.

With my purse draped across my body and my emergency tactical system (TACSAT) and handheld radio in my hands, I exited the office and secured the door, calling out a quick "Hey, is anybody here?" before securing the entire suite. Then I headed down the hall to exit the building and find out what happened.

Stepping over priceless artwork, overturned furniture, concrete, glass, and office supplies littering my path, I worked my way out of the classified section of the building to the catwalk that divided the building into two parts. *What in the hell happened?* I wondered. Not a living sound anywhere to be heard.

The catwalk separated the classified section of the embassy from the unclassified section. There was also an exit stairwell off of it. I was curious to see if there was life on the other side of the catwalk and to know if I could help in any manner before I dashed off to my house to bring the backup radio networks online. I knew security would have my head for still being inside, but I was in a crisis and uninjured, so my priority was to protect US government classified material before fleeing, which I did to the best of my ability. The altruistic side of me wanted to help anyone I could find, so I entered the unclassified part of the building.

"Oh my God!" I mumbled. I found no one in sight, but the devastation was shocking. The building's concrete perimeter walls facing the road were gone. From where I stood, I could see that only mangled steel and fragments of concrete remained. Furniture and boulders of concrete were tossed everywhere. Office supplies lined the floor. It was crazy!

"Is anyone there?" Silence.

"*Habari, habari. Dada . . . Kaka . . . Nina dada Vella.*" I called out to my colleagues, asking if anyone was there and identifying myself. More silence. Now I was truly mystified. What happened to my colleagues?

Is this real? Is it a dream? Am I dead? Is this the end of the world? Why am I the only one alive? My heart was racing, but my thoughts had a huge lead. I wiped the dusty sweat from my face and backed out toward the catwalk. I heard something hard fall behind the door and was glad it missed me.

The stairwell I had to take to get out of the building was lined with twisted metal, broken concrete, streaks of blood, and God knows what else. I maneuvered around the debris and managed to get to the bottom with only a few scratches and cuts to my arms and feet.

After I made it down the fragile stairs and went around the corner to exit the building, I encountered another shock: the route was blocked by a mound of debris—furniture, concrete, wire, metal, glass, etc. I was barricaded in. To make matters worse, a foul-smelling heat enveloped me, making me want to vomit. I propped my exhausted body on a fractured wall and screamed, "Hello!"

No answer.

"Hello!"

I took deep breaths to calm myself between calling out. My lungs burned, and my eyes had become coated in dust.

"Hello! Hello!"

"Who's back there?"

I stood up straight and screamed, "It's me, Vella! Help me!"

"Vella?"

"Yes, it's me, Vella!"

"Vella, climb up and give me your hand. Let's get you out of here!"

I carefully scaled the pile until I saw a Marine who worked at the embassy. He extended his hand, and I gave him my TACSAT. He took it and told me to grab his extended hand and use my other hand to crawl toward him. I did so, getting a few more scratches and cuts, but that was not an issue to me. I wanted to be out of that embassy and would crawl through fire if I had to.

On the other side of the pile, the familiar face hugged me and led me to a spiral stairwell that led to an exit door to the outside. Freedom! I never knew that path to the outside of the building existed. Thank God for it!

Outside, amid the destruction, I saw the Chargé d'Affaires (CDA) and other key country team members scurrying about. I became excited and knew it was my time to do what I was trained to do as a communications officer during a crisis. With my TACSAT in hand, I rushed toward the CDA to tell him that I was about to set up the TACSAT for him and the others to use. He directed me to join a group in a van on the other side of the perimeter wall so I could be taken to safety. I didn't ask questions or insist I put up my TACSAT, which I was dying to do. He was my leader, and I followed his orders.

"Why were you still in the building, Vella?" the management officer asked when I reached the perimeter wall.

"I was securing the communications center," I responded. I grabbed his hands for support as I headed up and over the wall.

After climbing into the van, I sat down a few rows in front of the new IMS. I had completely forgotten about her since she had just arrived the day before. Her shirt was bloody, and a small section of her nose was ripped and hanging.

"It's me, Vella," she said hoarsely.

"Yikes, are you OK?" I hesitantly replied. She nodded that she was.

I tested my handheld radio again. Still no feedback. The van drove off, and we were taken to the Deputy Chief of Mission's house to safety. After the last person jumped from the van, I asked the driver to take me to my house down the street.

"Dada, siwezi." *Sister, I can't*, he said in Swahili.

He told me in Swahili that he had to wait for instructions from the General Services Officer—his boss.

"Hamna shida kaka, nina elewa," I responded. *No worries brother, I understand.*

I did not have time to explain to him why I needed to go to my house. It would be faster to take a taxi.

So, with the TACSAT and radio in my hands, and my heavy purse still draped across my body, I ran toward Toure Drive. I waved at the first taxi I saw, and it stopped. I jumped in. He looked frightened as he looked over at me.

"Wapi?" *Where?*

"Drive, I will show you." The driver looked confused, so I added, "Gari, haraka, haraka!" *Drive, fast, fast!*

He punched the gas.

"Can you stay and be my driver for the rest of the day?" I asked him when he arrived at my house.

"Sawa, sawa, dada yangu." *OK, OK, my sister.*

Prologue: Discovery

I didn't know exactly what was going on, but I knew I needed to get the communications equipment back up and running, and I would do whatever it took to make it happen. Only later would I learn that suicide bombers detonated a truck full of explosives outside the embassy.

Their homemade bomb destroyed the embassy and snuffed out lives and dreams.

It *changed* lives.

It made me reassess my life.

In the midst of the chaos, terror, and uncertainty, I discovered who I was.

I was a US diplomat from the muddy roads of Holmestown, Georgia, and there was no other person or place on earth I would rather be.

CHAPTER 1

Dreams

Today brings me joy, for I am living it now.
I can't alter my past; it is done and gone.
I accept tomorrow as it unfolds, for it is my path.

I have always been a dreamer. One of my earliest memories is lying in the grass underneath a sprawling oak in our yard. I'd look up, up, up, between curvy limbs shimmering with lacy Spanish moss and silver-green leaves to the blue sky. There was no end in sight, and on a clear day, I could see forever. Most of the time, I could spot a white streak growing longer as if scribbled by an invisible hand. If I got lucky, I could see the glint of the airplane that made the white streak. I'd lie there in awe until the line grew faint then disappeared.

Who's up there in those planes? I wondered.

Where are they going?

Maybe Korea.

I had no idea where Korea was. I only knew it was far away. My dad and his buddies—old men from the community like Uncle Charlie, Jacob King, Hank Price, Mr. Felix, Mr. Harry Lee, and Mr. Mack Jones were the ones who came by regularly—would play cards, talk trash, and drink cold beer underneath that tree

1

on steamy summer afternoons and into the nights. They'd talk about past wars on foreign soil, gripe about what was happening to black folks in America, and strategize how to win from illegal gambling, better known as "Cuba."

If a plane happened to take off from nearby Fort Stewart Army Base, Jacob King, who had served in the Korean War, would try to guess what type of plane it was. My dad and the others would squint skyward while holding their cards close to their chests, so others would not see their hands. If I was nearby them playing, I would look up, too.

I couldn't have been more than 6 or 7 years old, but it did not stop me from daydreaming about where the planes were going, who was on them, and most of all, how I could get on them and go far away, too. The more I listened to Jacob King, who had traveled more than the others due to a stint in the military, the more I grew passionate about seeing the world, even if it was via the military.

Later, when my oldest brother, Douglas, a.k.a. "Dougie," joined the Air Force, I'd dream about Texas, Vietnam, and Thailand because those are the places he served and loved, and would talk about the most when he visited home. He'd bring me a little something every time he came home from traveling: a red handkerchief from Texas or a wood-carved pencil from Thailand. I wasn't sure where some of these places were, but Dougie told me stories. He said the women in Texas were tall and thick and wore cowboy boots that pointed a mile out. I had no idea back then what cowboy boots were. We barely had worn-out shoes to wear. The Thailand stories intrigued me because he always talked about the canals, elephants, monkeys, pretty women, and abundance of seafood—some that had no name.

However, the most captivating and interesting stories were about the time he spent in Vietnam. With glossy eyes, he used to tell me how he walked through jungles with his soldier buddies and his gun. Whenever they came upon a city, he was most afraid of the kids and women because some carried explosives and knew how to shoot guns. He had to treat them like enemies in combat. I was horrified at what he told me, but I wanted to hear more and more.

Dougie was the first of my siblings to travel the world. Next was Ronald—the daredevil and dreamer like me. He joined the Army. Ryan, Ronald's twin, joined the army, too, followed by Steven, and then my baby brother, Eugene Jr., who we call "Junior." In fact, all my brothers joined the military, except Harold.

As my dad's gambling and drinking buddies grew older and riddled with knee problems or arthritis, they did not come around much, so I longed for my brothers to come home more frequently to share their worldly experiences. My sisters did not travel far, but they had broken away from my mother's chain and had either gotten married or gone to college a few counties away. As for me, I dreamed of being far away. It wasn't about getting away from my mother's chain, as it was about seeing what was beyond Holmestown.

By the time I was in high school, I'd had enough of being left behind. My siblings were coming and going, talking about the people they met at the Georgia Ball, at their college or trade school, in the military, on their vacation, in the friendly blue skies above, and everything else they had seen or done. It was the curse of being one of the youngest; I could only listen and dream, for now.

While my girlfriends dreamed of getting married to a rich or handsome man and having nice things, working at local schools and banks and hospitals, and raising kids, I dreamed of traveling the world, only returning to visit and share my experience with whoever would listen. I read books to escape Holmestown and the stifling hot air of my momma's non-air-conditioned house. I would take two or three books from the maroon-colored encyclopedia set my parents had purchased for us, then I would read them as I lay on the grass under the big oak tree in the backyard. I would flip through the pages to find pictures and stories of foreign places and people. I loved reading about them, but it also made me anxious; I needed a real plan to get to those places and people. I had nothing except a dream.

I felt stuck.

"Girl, you daydream too much. You better daydream about how you will make it in life because times are hard for black folks and will get worse by the time you are of age," my momma would say when she saw me reading those books or when I asked her if she knew where a particular place was. "Why do you want to know? Just read the book and get something in that picky head of yours to be somebody one day," she would say. That made me even more curious, so I would just sigh and go back to my tree to read and dream some more.

By the time I was approaching my last year in high school, I'd vowed to leave, come hell or high water—I was going to be on those big white planes that soared the beautiful blue skies. I could only imagine the big world out there, and once I got my education, I didn't want to dream about it. I wanted to see it, smell it, live it. I pictured myself dressed up in a black suit and white blouse, with long shiny black hair and shiny pumps. I carried a briefcase, and as I ran beside my boss, a sharp-dressed white man, through an airport on the way to somewhere—anywhere—I'd be taking notes. Yes, that was one of my most memorable dreams of being successful.

I would be a secretary. Coincidentally, that is the prediction my classmates made for me upon graduation—being a secretary at Bradwell Institute, the high school I graduated from. I would be important. Even if I were to be a secretary, it would be far away and for an important person, thus I would be important, too. That was my plan at the time. Because studying had always come easy, college seemed like the best way to make my exit. It seemed doable. Several of my sisters had gone to college or trade school, and two had graduated. Yet despite that and the fact that I was a member of the Beta Club, a prestigious high school club, my school counselor was not too helpful and seemed a little surprised that an underprivileged girl like me would even dream about going to college. If it weren't for my sisters who were already in college or had graduated, as well as my faith and dream, and my parents' determination for all their kids to make it in life, I would have given up. That counselor's actions, looks, and words were very discouraging to me. If I were to translate them, the message to me would have been: "Child, your family is poor. A picky-head girl like you from a poor family has no business considering such a lofty, expensive goal. Get a job locally. Get married and have babies. Your parents are already struggling from sending your other sisters to college as if they were rich."

Leave this woman's office. Get a job and be happy. This is what I was thinking when I left her office, as uninformed as when I entered it. I felt so weighed down, I could have sunk right into the ground.

What made me snap out of it and kept those thoughts out of my head was what I saw one day when I was passing by the counselor's office: several students who were poor academic performers, a few of whom I helped with their coursework on a regular basis, waiting to talk to a counselor about college. *Oh, hell no!* I thought. *My parents may not have a lot of money, but I am smart, and I want to go to college, and I will go to college. I just need to figure it out.*

I may have been poor, but I *mattered*! My momma had made sure of it. Sometimes when she caught me daydreaming, she used to say, "I hope that dream that's making you smile so much is a good one for your life and comes true one day." With no more than an eighth-grade education herself, she encouraged us to dream big, and she plastered inspirational posters and plaques all over our house to make sure we got the message and were equipped to overcome the obstacles we were surely going to encounter along the way. Even now, I remember one that hung in our living room over the wall-mounted telephone and is probably buried in the back room of relics she hoards as priceless to the family:

When things seem the hardest
or the worst
is when one should
hold on the tightest and
not let go
because God
will make a way
out of the seemingly impossible.

There was no use talking to that counselor—I'd show her that I was good enough, that I belonged. I would make my own dreams come true, starting right then.

Dreams

I enrolled at Albany State College and did my freshman year there. The money part just worked out somehow. My sister Brittany was there as a sophomore. We had fun attending the same college. However, when Momma used to call my dorm and not find me, she figured I was up to no good. After numerous episodes of not finding me, she made me transfer, as a sophomore, to Georgia Southern College in Statesboro. It was only 67 miles down the road from home, but still a world away from Holmestown.

It did not matter where I went to college, as long as I went, because I knew that attending college was putting me on the path to achieving my dream of seeing the world. Actually, my dream had started materializing the minute I left Holmestown for college, because I was in a part of Georgia I had never seen, and I traveled to outlying counties for extracurricular activities or to sightsee. I was exploring the world beyond Holmestown and loving it. Being in predominately white Statesboro at Georgia Southern College was like being in France or the United Arab Emirates—there was a different thought pattern, and even the dialects were different than mine. But all of us students had common goals: to graduate and begin making our dreams come true while having fun. I did both.

School came easy to me, so I had time to spare. Natalie, one of my best friends at Georgia Southern College, encouraged me to pledge Alpha Kappa Alpha sorority with her during our junior year. I wasn't sure at first, but I discussed it with my sister Emma, who had already graduated from nursing school, and she was excited about me doing it, so I did. Pledging was not as harsh as it is now, but it was still torture being told when to eat, sleep, study, and sometimes talk/socialize. I went to college to grow into my own and become a leader, not to be a follower, talked down to by the big sisters of the sorority for the entire three months of pledging. If it weren't for my friend and my other sorority sisters, I probably would have dropped out, but they encouraged me to stick it out.

My experience as an Ivy pledge for that sorority taught me patience, tolerance, and persistence, as well as how to be a follower and leader, how to be a team player, and how to suavely maneuver obstacles. For example, even though I pledged, I had to study— Lord, did they ensure we studied—but there wasn't enough time in the day with all the sorority activities to maintain my excellent grades. I had to think—and think fast—before my grades fell. So, I used to fake being sick to go to my room to get some extra studying in. If I recall accurately, I had the highest GPA that semester of anyone in the Ivy crossover to sisterhood. So, I got both—good grades and my sorority pin. Who said if you dream it, it can come true? I had seen twice now that I knew how to intelligently maneuver obstacles to get what I wanted.

I wasn't alone in making things happen. From my strong attendance at St. Peter's African Methodist Episcopal (AME) church, I learned that there is power in the word of Jesus. So, I spoke his name as often as I could, especially when I was facing tough situations or crossroads. Being poor with big dreams and strict parents, I had to call on Jesus a lot. I wanted to stay on course and not stray too much. Even when I wasn't in bad situations, by calling his name often via songs and simply thanking him for the smallest of blessings, I felt his presence. That feeling made me know he was always with me no matter where I went.

In keeping with my faith, I would attend college campus Bible study as often as I could. Singing the old-time spiritual hymns from the top of my lungs before and after the sessions was so cleansing to me. I felt revived—and still do—after singing them.

I have always been a spiritual person, but I began to believe even more deeply in the power of prayer while in college. One night in particular, I was sleepless and weary because I wanted so much to make an "A" on a final exam to make the dean's list again. My grades were decent, but not like the semester before, so I was worried and doubting. My heart was racing fast, and I knew I would not sleep unless I could calm it. Naturally, I fell to my knees with locked hands and started praying. I felt relaxed, but I needed something more. I rolled out of bed and got my Bible from my desk across the room. I turned to the book of Mark, Chapter 11, and read one of my favorite stories in the Bible—Jesus' cursing of the fig tree. The story goes that while Jesus was on a journey with followers, he cursed a barren fig tree and it died soon after. I am no scholar of the Bible, but I believe that Jesus used this as an example to show his followers that whatever they prayed for, as long as they had faith that they would receive it, it would be theirs. I wanted to make the dean's list. The words of that story encouraged me to have faith and believe it would happen. I placed the Bible on my chest, thinking, metaphorically, that if there was any doubt in my faith that I would make the dean's list, the words from the Bible lying on my chest would go directly into my heart and change it. If that didn't work, the next day I would fall to my knees and pray again.

When I awoke the next morning, my Bible was lying on the other side of the room, face up on the floor and still on the page I was reading. I hadn't moved it. My roommate said she hadn't either.

I took it as a sign. *Prayer is powerful*, I thought. *God is real. God is with me no matter how far away he may seem. He cares about me and will take care of things for me, but in his own time, not mine. And if I pray and believe, I will receive what I am praying for!*

I kept this realization close in my heart as I moved toward graduation. I wasn't sure where I was going, but I knew that God would go with me, and if I ever doubted his powers, I needed to do nothing more than to call his name, pray, and read my favorite verses in the book of Mark from the worn-out Bible Momma gave me when I left for college. Truth be known, those verses still move mountains and cause locked doors to open for me.

The funny thing about dreams is that they never happen when you expect them. Straight out of college, I moved to Monterey, California, where my brother Ryan lived. Almost immediately, I landed a job using my business degree. The transition was smooth, and I assumed it would be the same for fitting together all the puzzle pieces of my life to create the future I imagined. But nobody told me how easy it would be to get distracted— especially when the distraction came in the form of a good-looking man.

I had no trouble dating, and in California, I was pleasantly surprised to find that it was a free-for-all. Color made no difference. If you were single, anyone was fair game. I quickly became involved with a white army officer who was not only handsome, but kind and gentle, with no color hang-ups. Looking back, I most likely would have married him had Ryan, whom I was living with, not discouraged our relationship. Ryan was not so keen on his little sister dating a white guy or a commissioned officer, or maybe both. Who knows. All I know is that I liked the guy but had to cut the relationship short because it displeased my brother. Back then, pleasing my family meant more to me than my happiness.

Bending to Ryan's wishes, I began dating Tim Perry, a friend of his and a soldier in his squadron on the Fort Ord Army Base, where he was assigned. I resisted initially, mainly because, unlike the officer, he had nothing intellectual to offer me. Also, he didn't look or act like the man of my dreams. Eventually, when it seemed like my brother was cutting me off from another guy I befriended, I decided to go out with Tim. *At least he has a job*, I thought.

He took me to nice restaurants. He bought me nice gifts. He enjoyed showing me off. "This is my beautiful Georgia girl who has a college degree," he would brag to friends and colleagues. Yes, he had some flattering names for me, and I started to enjoy being around him more and more. Before long, we were an item. I couldn't believe my luck! Here I was, a 23-year-old young woman from Georgia living in California with a great job and a boyfriend who was born and raised in Riceville, just 30 minutes from Holmestown. How lucky I was—or so I thought. I reveled in the attention he lavished on me.

In a whirlwind, we married, but instead of walking down the aisle, I should have walked away—or run away, and fast. His domineering nature revealed itself on our wedding day when he tried to force me to remove my makeup before the ceremony. He was not even supposed to see me, but he barged into the room. After the reception that evening, he refused to go on our honeymoon and talked cruelly to me in front of his friends. I had just said "I do," but I already knew the marriage wouldn't last after hearing his cruel words to me in public. Yet being me, ever confident and optimistic, I figured I could hold on for a few years so my family and friends would not ask too many questions as to why I got a divorce after being married for such a short period. Also, I stayed with Tim out of respect for my brother—I did not want him to feel bad about hooking me up with a dud.

Soon after the wedding, I became pregnant. Our son, Andrew, was born in the fall of 1983. From the start, motherhood was too much for me to bear, especially so far away from my momma and sisters. Oh yes, I wanted Momma then. Andrew was fragile and so was I because he was born two months early, and I was overwhelmed by the responsibilities of being a working mother to an infant who required special care. Sensing that I was near my breaking point, I asked my sister Rachel to come to California to help me for a while. She did. While she helped me, she also saw the condition of the marriage, but she kept her mouth shut except to teach me how to "cope," or maybe I should say "survive." When her time was up, I asked her to take the baby back to Georgia with her until I could break away and move from California, or at least until I felt strong enough to raise him myself. Waving at my fragile baby boy and sister as they got in the car with friends of my brothers from Alabama to drive 3,000 miles away was the most painful thing I had done up to that point in my life. I would have never done it if I had been strong enough to make the marriage work or put fear in my husband when he wanted to fight me about frivolous things. I needed my child to be safe and not experience what I used to as a child when I heard and saw Momma and Daddy fussing and fighting weekend after weekend. Those days haunted me (and still do), and I did not want it for Andrew. He had to go away while I handled my business with his father, but I promised him when I kissed him goodbye that I would come to get him soon.

Complicating the situation, Tim had transfer orders to move to an assignment in the Sinai Peninsula. I was happy that I could not go with him—I figured it was my way back to my son and possibly the beginning of the end of the marriage.

When Tim left for his assignment, I moved back to Georgia and got a job at Fort Stewart working in the Army Corps of Engineers office. My parents' home was less than 10 minutes from the military base, so naturally, since I had a small child and very little money at the time, I stayed with them. It was not a good setup, but it was temporary.

When Tim returned from the Sinai and transferred to Fort Bragg in North Carolina, he suggested making amends. Tired of living under my parents' roof, I transferred my job to the Fort Bragg Army Corps of Engineers office and joined Tim there. But it was no use. Tim hadn't changed; in fact, his abuse grew worse. He never took me and the baby anywhere, and when I went somewhere alone, he would accuse me of meeting men. If I stayed anywhere longer than what he perceived as normal, I came home to the big three—fists, fights, and fusses. Andrew started crying more during the episodes, but it didn't faze his dad. *Stupid me*, I thought. *Why did I leave my parents' house to try to give the marriage a second chance with this man?* It just was not happening—there would be no reconciliation, so I started planning my escape out of the marriage.

Well, one must always be careful what they ask God for. I was indeed going to be delivered out of the marriage—but almost in a body bag. Late one night when we were about to go back to Fort Bragg after visiting family in Georgia, Tim showed Juan, my brother-in-law, who was New York cop, a gun in the trunk of our car and told him that he was going to blow my head off and throw me in the woods along the way if I gave him any crap about arriving late to get me and the baby. Juan, being a seasoned cop, acted quickly and discreetly to get the gun from Tim and to convince me not to take the long trip that late at night. After that incident, I only returned to Fort Bragg once more. With my sister Rachel's help, I went there and got my and my baby's belongings out of the trailer we had been living in. While we were there, one of the last things I needed to do was to approach Tim at his job to get the keys to our vehicle. I had our child and needed to have the vehicle. Even knowing that, he spat in my face and only relinquished the keys to the car after his commander told him to do so. The spit was so fierce coming out of his mouth and onto my face that it splattered onto Rachel's and his commander's faces. Nasty! Tim Perry was just plain nasty, and I had no room in my life for this type of person.

It seems ludicrous that someone would return willingly to an abusive relationship, but I realized the importance of having my father in my life, and I wanted the same for my son. That's why I went to Fort Bragg with my husband in the first place. In spite of rocky times, my parents had managed to stay together. In fact, my dad died in my mom's arms. Until death do us part—how tearfully sweet. I would have loved to have kept my vows, but I did not want to kill Tim or be killed by him. Most important, I did not want our son to be harmed in the cross fire, emotionally or physically. I did not consider myself a quitter back then, but staying married was asking for trouble—and in a big way. I knew I would leave him, but I didn't want to give up without trying to make it work. Then reality slapped me in the face—or should I say spit in my face. Less than a year after I stood with Tim's nasty phlegm on my face, humiliated and angry, the divorce proceedings were complete, and the marriage was over for good.

After Tim spit on me that day, I drove off in my car down Interstate 95 with Rachel trailing me in her car. Once again, I ended up at my parents' house in Holmestown, destitute. For the first time in my life, I didn't have a plan. I didn't have a job. My parents were less than thrilled with my situation, and Momma made no attempts to hide her disappointment. I couldn't blame her. I was disappointed in myself. Nevertheless, I did not give up.

One day after coming from a job interview at Fort Stewart, I saw a "Help Wanted" sign at Grab-a-Bag, a convenience store and gas station near our family's church and a busy intersection. I inquired and was hired on the spot—it was my lucky day! It did not occur to me that Grab-a-Bag is where everyone stopped for gas or a quick snack. Having boasted about going to college and leaving Georgia, here I was with no husband, a baby, no sign of an interesting and exciting future, and too defeated to dare dream about getting far away from Holmestown again. It was no secret that the old classmates I saw almost daily made fun of me—a cashier with a college degree. I was humiliated, but I sucked it up with a smile and said nothing. My faith kicked in, and I prayed. Praying delivered two opportunities at once: a job offer at Fort Stewart as a management assistant and an acceptance letter from a college in Atlanta to pursue my MBA.

I discussed my dilemma with my sister Emma, who really wanted me to get my master's degree. My son, Andrew, barely 2 years old, was there during the discussion, playing around my legs, and for a quick second, our eyes locked. I could not leave him. I explained to Emma why this was not an ideal time for me to go back to college. Although she offered to keep Andrew for me and raise him as her own while I was in college, I did not want to leave him with anyone. I needed to be with my baby boy. I wanted to ensure he did not turn out like his father. I wanted to see him as his father's traits appeared and teach him a different way. He had to be a better person than his father, and I wanted him to be successful. I wanted a hand in it all for my baby boy! So, I accepted the job offer at Fort Stewart.

Good ol' Fort Stewart, always there for me. But, Lord, being around military folks and their foreign spouses awakened the travel bug in me again—something I thought was dead and gone. Fishing for opportunities, I went to the library to peruse any publications that listed job openings. If my memory serves me correctly, I believe the *Federal Jobs Digest* was the one that I liked the most. So, I selected 50 interesting positions and used my lunch money for the week to copy applications and mail them out—there was no internet back then. Most were sent to military bases, but I also cast my net wide, sending applications to various government agencies in Washington, DC, including the US Department of State Foreign Service, whatever that was.

One by one, I was weeded out—lack of experience, more qualified applicants, location, and so forth. The repeated rejections were disheartening. *Would I ever leave Holmestown again?* My faith remained strong, but I did not know when God would deliver! Daily, I read my favorite chapter in the book of Mark and thought about how I woke up to the Bible on the floor while in college. That lifted my spirits. I knew I just had to keep my hopes higher than the planes I saw in the blue skies above and keep my eyes open for opportunities. Oh, and continue to pray!

In the process of trying to get a job back in California at Fort Ord, I hooked up romantically with a Native American man, "Papa

Big Thunder," in the human resources office out there. Yes, a man again—offering me a way out of my current life. My son and I visited him frequently in California while I patiently waited to be offered a position from the numerous applications I sent out. The offer never came. Before long, Papa Big Thunder accepted a human resources officer position at one of the military bases in Japan, and off he went. I later joined him to try my luck there, this time leaving my son with my momma until I could return to bring him back to live with me in Japan. Once again, on my own, I saw the real man. That seemingly nice man slammed me into a closet door when I defied his orders not to befriend black men at the base. I was on the next flight to Holmestown—back at my parents' house and glad to be reunited with my son. Strike three. I gave up trying to do it on my own. *It's up to you, God. Jesus, speak to your father, our father for me, please, sir.* I prayed. After everything that I had been through since college, I thought God was not hearing me, so I had to call on Jesus to intercede on my behalf.

Thank goodness I had sense enough to take leave from my job instead of quitting when I joined Papa Big Thunder in Japan, or else I would have been looking for a job again. I returned to my job as a management assistant at Fort Stewart. I was a smart lady.

About a year later, there was a mass movement of personnel from Fort Stewart to the new Naval Submarine Base Kings Bay in St. Marys, Georgia, about 45 minutes from my parents' home. I applied, naturally. While waiting for something to transpire, I continued receiving information requests from the Department of State in Washington, DC, for one of the 50 positions I had originally applied for. Finally, I was called for an interview—the Oral Assessment is the official name for it.

Around that time, I was in a relationship with Thomas Brown (I called him Tommie), and he helped me prepare for the Oral Assessment. He knew current events and drilled me about things we believed I would be asked—world events, our government, etc. He had body and brains. I didn't care if I passed or not. I was in love again.

Well, my love was strong for Tommie, but not enough to weaken my performance in the interview. I went to Washington, DC, for the first time, alone on a cold and snowy winter day, and I passed the Oral Assessment with flying colors. I was given a conditional offer of employment for the Department of State Foreign Service, contingent upon passing a medical examination and suitability review, and obtaining top-secret clearance—a process they told me could take a year or more, depending on my background and medical condition. This little girl from Holmestown had no idea what she was getting into—and I didn't have time to think about it. I was pumped up about the prospect of moving away from Holmestown again, even if I was in love with someone there. And I did like that thick piece of chocolate man from Louisiana.

Help me, Lord. Once again, a man came along to distract me from my path. I really had to focus on my career this time, despite how much I believed I was in love with Tommie. I really thought Tommie could have been the One.

My cousin Jake introduced me to him. They were both in the same squadron at Fort Stewart. When I saw that hunk of chocolate drive by one day as I was walking from my trailer home to my momma's house for exercise, I had to turn around to look again. *A hunk of dark chocolate driving a BMW. Yummy and looking good!* I smiled and went from a fast walk to a sexy jog to get my mind

18

off what I had just seen. Within minutes, he had turned around and pulled up beside me in his black BMW. I slowed down to a fast walk again. Cousin Jake was in the passenger seat with a big smile on his face. He introduced us, and when Tommie spoke, I noticed the dimples and I started acting like a high school girl being asked to prom. Cousin Jake saw the sparks, so he asked Tommie to take him home just down the street and come back to talk to me. Tommie did just that. When he returned, he drove slowly as I did a sexy girl jog again. We were both hooked at first sight and chatted ourselves into a friendship. Like my now ex-husband, Tim, Tommie was a military man with a few dollars in his pocket. He wasted no time wooing me with flowers, chocolate, movies, and fine drinks. The material things did not flatter me too much, but knowing that he had the means of showering me with gifts was appealing.

Even though I loved being with Tommie and how he supported my career endeavors, he was still black and in the military, and that combination of things did not work for me in the past. However, he was gorgeous and drove a nice, reliable car. But deep in my heart I knew it would not last, and I knew my momma would kill me if I married another soldier. So, I focused on my job search while trying to enjoy Tommie for the period God sent him to me. But I made it clear that I wouldn't marry him. The more I pushed him away, the harder and sweeter he came at me. Fortunately, after I had passed the Oral Assessment, I also learned that I had landed the job at the Kings Bay Submarine Base. I was happy because that put distance between us, and between me and Holmestown, yet again.

After an attempt at a long-distance relationship, Tommie decided to leave the military and move in with me while he looked for a job at the base as a civilian. However, he had a few months to go, so he and I picked out a great apartment and he helped me move in one summer. The first night in the apartment, Tommie and I had a great time. He bought me chocolate and a bottle of Dom Pérignon champagne. I had never heard of it, but I knew it was costly. *Wow, all for me.* It came at a price, a high price. The champagne deeply affected my cognitive ability.

The next morning, I woke up with a ring on my finger and the vague recollection of an old white man pronouncing us man and wife.

"Tommie, what happened, and why do I have a ring on my finger?" I whispered while holding my head.

"You finally said 'yes,' baby," he said. He showed me a document that had my signature on it. It seemed to say we got married by a justice of the peace just down the road in O'Neil, Georgia.

My heart stopped. I felt ashamed. I felt dirty. I felt stupid. I wanted to cry, take the ring off, and go away for good. It was no use.

I was stuck. The honeymoon ended before it started because he had to return to work the next day. I did not want to be alone in the apartment because I did not want to have too much time on my hands to think about the horrible mistake I made. So, I had Frank, Rachel's son who was one of my favorite nephews, stay with me until Tommie moved in permanently in a few months. It was summertime, so he had nothing much to do in Holmestown. He was great company to distract me, and since then, he and I have had a great and respectful relationship.

Soon after Frank returned to Holmestown for school, Tommie's stint in the military ended, and it was time for me to face the music of seeing my husband every day. It was scary because I did not really know how he would be as a spouse on a daily basis. *Was he going to be as sweet as he looked?* I wondered. *Was I going to have to fight him constantly like I did with Tim Perry? Was he truly going to be supportive of my dreams to travel the world?* Lord have mercy, now I was a wife, a mother to Andrew, and the only breadwinner in the family.

Well, Tommie lost no time seeking employment. He set out to find a job as a diesel mechanic. He had plenty of experience—he earned his mechanic's license in the military—but few garages bothered to call him back, and there was nothing on the naval base for him at that time. He even expanded his search to nearby Jacksonville, Florida, but with no luck.

Things were dismal for Tommie taking control of our family as the provider. Since he couldn't find a job, he grew depressed and angrier by the day. He cared for Andrew, did the shopping and cleaning, and prepared meals when he was not job seeking. But this was not his forte—he hated it, and I felt it.

He was just not happy with his role of being a "Mr. Mom," as he used to jokingly refer to himself. Eventually, things turned bad. He'd disappear during the day, leaving my baby boy with a nice old lady who used to watch him when I needed a babysitter. If I found out and asked where he went, he would tell me not to ask him questions because he was the man of the family, not me. The first time he said this, I felt a sinking feeling in my stomach, just like when I heard Tim's response when I asked him to leave his friends so we could depart for our honeymoon. That was the "blood red" flag for me that I was in trouble, again. Nevertheless, I wanted to make the marriage work. I did not want another failed marriage.

Occasionally, I'd wake up and he'd be gone. Sometimes I'd find him sitting on the trailer-home steps looking up at the starry sky. Day after day, he distanced himself from me, but he held on at the same time. He did not want to be lovey-dovey or talk like we used to, but he did not want me too far away from him. I'd walk out of work in the afternoons to find him in the parking lot, watching to see who I talked to or walked with to my car. He'd hide behind the shelves at the Winn-Dixie grocery store, where I worked part-time, spying on me. If a man laughed and smiled with me as I processed his grocery order at the checkout counter, Tommie would suddenly appear with a loaf of bread, a canned good, or whatever he could find and tell the guy he needed to move on because he was in a rush. Back then, I called him crazy in love, but now I realize that my own husband stalked me.

Yes, just like my first husband, Tommie grew possessive. At home, if I dared leave for an errand, he'd spit on the ground and warn me to be back before it dried. I questioned myself about what had changed in our relationship to bring about the shift in behavior, and the only answer I could fathom is that his pride was wounded as he saw me progress while he could not find work. I had a good job and he had none. I was the breadwinner and he made dinner. Tommie was manly, and being in this situation was a big blow to his ego. That is what went wrong!

Having been through this before, I could handle whatever he threw at me personally, but my patience grew thin when I realized his interaction with my son was not like it used to be. A mother knows this, even if she doesn't witness it. To ensure my son was not subjected to Tommie's negativity too much, I began taking Andrew with me whenever I could. The red flag was still waving in front of me, and I began looking for a way out. I needed to be free in the marriage, and my son needed a loving man to help raise him.

Money problems exacerbated our issues. The guy who once lavished me with gifts now had to live off my earnings. He called me controlling when I told him not to spend so much on unnecessary things. I resented him spending my hard-earned money frivolously—on alcohol, unnecessary clothes, upgrades to his BMW. We needed to save, and he spent like there was no bottom in my purse.

One morning after I came home from working the night shift at the submarine base, Tommie and Andrew were nowhere in sight. The BMW was gone. Tommie's clothes and the TV were gone. Some of the antiques he collected when he was in Germany were gone. We did not have cell phones back then. Frantically, I called his friends' home numbers, and they had not heard from him. I called his mom in Louisiana and learned that after taking my son to the babysitter, he had returned home to Louisiana in the middle of the night. I asked to speak to him, but he refused to come to the phone. *Why did he just up and leave in the middle of the night? What a coward,* I thought. I rushed over to the babysitter to get my son and checked him to see if he was OK. He was, but I could not sleep, as I often did during the day after being on the night shift. I needed answers from Tommie. I guess my Libra traits kicked in. My scale would forever be tipped if I did not fix the relationship or end it properly.

So, I called my ex-husband, Tim, who was now out of the military and back in Riceville, Georgia, to ask him to keep our little boy so I could drive to Louisiana to get answers. I had to tell him what happened. I drove to Riceville to drop Andrew off and then back to Florida to reach Highway 10 before heading west to

Pierre, Louisiana. It was a long road trip, but I was manic and could have driven to the moon and back if I had to. Finally, I arrived in his hometown. I went straight to his mother's house, where I found him. I pleaded, cried, even screamed at him for disappearing without leaving so much as a note with an explanation. His parents and siblings were nearby, listening with a look on their faces I could not interpret.

"I can't be married to a bossy and controlling woman, to a woman who makes more money than I do," he said. "In my family, my dad is the man of the house. I need to be the man of my house." He looked at his dad and said, "Tell her, Dad. We Brown men take care of our family."

His dad dropped his gaze and did not say anything except, "Well, son."

I understood Tommie's feelings, truly I did, but I needed him to understand that while I did not mind him using our money, he had to be more cognizant of how he spent the little we had. "If we're just a little thriftier," I said, "surely we can work through this period until you find work. I can take another look at your résumé or ask around about mechanic jobs in Riceville. I can even move here to Louisiana if you think there are more opportunities here." I held my breath slightly as I said that one—*oh God, move to Louisiana?* I racked my brains trying to come up with solutions that he would buy into. We talked for hours, and when I finally fell asleep in his arms, I felt confident that we'd patched things up.

The next morning, the first thing I said was, "Come on, babe, let's go home and execute our plan to get you working again."

He looked at me as if I were stupid. He snarled and said, "You must be crazy. I am not staying in this marriage with you."

I felt weak. I should have immediately said, "I tried. Good riddance. I am out!" since it was the perfect opportunity to end the marriage. However, I felt sorry for him and wanted him to be on his feet with a decent job before I closed the door on the marriage. That is the kindness in me, I suppose.

I stood in shock. Tommie then picked up the house cordless phone. He walked away and spoke very quietly with a smile on his face. I had no idea who he had called until he handed me the phone and said, "Here, talk to the woman who will really be my wife. We're getting married once I divorce you." My heart dropped, but he was here with me, not her, and I was still the wife, so I felt I had the upper hand. I hung up the phone without speaking into it.

"Please, Tommie, let's talk about it!" I cried, sobbing. I rushed to him and grabbed on, begging him to come back with me.

"Stop it! Don't you get it? I don't want to be with you anymore! I don't want *you* anymore!"

Tommie shoved me out the front door of his parents' house. It was raining, and I slipped on the wet stairs. In the same way that he'd drag an overstuffed trash bag out to the curb, he grabbed my shirt and dragged me through the mud to my car.

"It's over, woman. Get that through your head, OK?" He turned around and went inside his parents' house.

I laid there in disbelief before slowly coming to my feet and crawling into the car. I was embarrassed beyond imagination. Soaked and dirty from the muddy road, I sat and cried, then glanced up. His parents and siblings were now standing on the porch looking sorry for me, but they did not say anything. Tommie was looking through the window from inside the house.

I slowly turned the ignition key, hit the gas, and headed home.

———————————

I am embarrassed now to think about how much of my self-worth was wrapped up in that loser of a man. I had vowed to never let a man control me, much less my heart, and the realization that it had happened not once, or twice, but three times, confounded me. Yet despite the imbalanced, difficult dynamics of our relationship, I had cared deeply for Tommie. Once again, I had failed at making a man see me for me and not the enemy, and that realization left me empty and raw.

In the days following our breakup, I went through the motions of working and caring for my son, but with little to look forward to. My family was about an hour away—too far to rely on for day-to-day support without tying up their phone lines talking for hours. So, I went within myself. I prayed and read my Bible. I asked God to help me. Help me in what way? I did not know; I was too screwed up to know what to ask for, so I just asked him to help me.

My dream of traveling is gone, and this time for good, I thought.

At that point in my life, I only wanted to focus on two things: being a superb mother to Andrew and excelling in the workplace, since I figured I would be there until I eventually retired. My fire and enthusiasm for traveling around the world and experiencing amazing things were gone.

Months went by and I started finding solace in a colleague, an older white man from up north who befriended me. I still remember his name and how he looked. He lent an ear to my never-ending stories. He provided an outlet for me when everything seemed overwhelming. Oh, and he was handsome and kind, too!

Our supervisor, Judy, had spent her entire life in the South. She made no effort to hide her prejudice toward blacks. The idea of blacks and whites mingling on a social level was unacceptable to her. She was especially resentful of me, an attractive, college-educated black woman who was liked by all—black and white. I could tell she was waiting for me to screw up so she could fire me. She was always watching me, so I laid low as much as possible. However, I could not resist being around my colleague who listened to me. He was becoming attractive to me. In my head, I knew it wasn't a good idea to get involved with him, but my heart had other ideas.

To distract myself, I visited my parents and siblings a lot. I sat around not saying much to them because I honestly do not believe they would have understood my complicated life.

My mother, never one for pitying us, didn't understand my dark mood, but she knew I was in a dark place.

"Girl, what do you want to do with your life?" she asked me one day when I told her that I was waiting on a job in Washington, DC. I had no idea if the job would ever materialize, but it sounded good and even hopeful.

"I want to travel, a lot."

"Well, then travel. Do whatever you want to do, but don't forget that you have a son you have to take care of."

Andrew had to be taken care of, but at times I felt like I needed to be taken care of more than that little baby boy. I wanted so much for him, but with the pressures of being a single parent, working through the healing process for my broken heart, and dealing with an unfair supervisor, I was drowning.

One night on the job (I had the night shift that week), I struggled to pull myself together. I was the epitome of a depressed person. "Keep your head up, Vella," my white male friend said as I walked slowly past him with my head hung down. He grabbed my hands, pulled me into his arms, gave me a big hug, and patted me on the back—just as my supervisor Judy rounded the corner. Jumping at the chance to reprimand me, she accused me of inappropriate workplace behavior and told me she would proceed with terminating me the next day. I looked at her in shock. *What did I do? I was not doing the hugging and patting. It was my white friend!* These objections ran through my head, but I was too depressed to argue with her. I shed a few tears, pushed out of his arms, and slowly walked to the bathroom with my head still low. *I guess that is what it comes down to,* I thought as I looked at the pitiful sight in the mirror. *I am screwed!*

When morning came and my shift was over, the word was out that I was going to be terminated for showing affection in the workplace. I left the office that stuffy, hot morning with my head still low, but this time in a mixture of depression and shame. The same white guy walked me to the car and told me to keep my head high—it will be OK, he said. I smiled, but inside I had hit bottom. Wallowing in self-pity, I went home and pulled a six-pack out of the refrigerator with every intention of drinking myself to sleep or to death.

What have I done wrong, God? I asked.

I dropped to my knees and pleaded my case.

Why me? How am I going to get through this crisis? I'm barely making ends meet with a full-time job—there's no way I'll survive without one. Just tell me what to do because I'm out of plans and ideas.

As I was still kneeling and sobbing in my hands after speaking to God, the phone rang.

When I answered it, a voice on the other end said, "Vella, I am calling from the US Department of State in Washington, DC. We'd like to officially offer you a slot in the next new-hire class as a Support Communications Officer with the Foreign Service."

God? Did I hear what I think I heard?

"Ma'am, please, please do not joke with me," I said.

"I'm not. If you're willing to accept, you can join a class beginning in two weeks or wait for the next class in several months. Which do you prefer?"

Dizzy from the thought of how quickly God responded, I said, "In two weeks."

She laughed and said, "What's the rush?"

I spent the next few minutes spewing every detail from the last six months of my life into the phone.

"You can't get fired—it will mean less pay when we bring you on board at the Department of State," she said. "Thank God for your blessing, then get off your knees and go back immediately to the office and resign."

I couldn't believe my ears. I couldn't believe that God had answered my prayer with such a direct, immediate, definitive answer. Any doubt about his hand in my life vanished.

I went straight to the office and resigned. Thank goodness I reached human resources before ol' Judy did. She thought she had me, so she took her time getting around to putting in the paperwork.

My resignation was accepted. There, I was done! I was free, and my dream was on again. I was going places!

If I could go back in time and speak with the skinned-knee, hell-raising, defiant, pigtailed girl who daydreamed underneath the oak tree, I'd tell her to keep dreaming and to not be discouraged by anyone calling her a dreamer. Dream on, and dream big. Dream often. Dream when you can't see any tangible way for your dreams to come true. Having the luxury of living out my dreams, I've learned that, above all, they require patience and perseverance. It's not enough to wish for something: You must doggedly chase it down every day, even when you don't feel like it.

In my early adult life, I got sidetracked by men and what I thought was love, but in my gut, I knew that I wasn't supposed to be in those marriages for long. They were too confining for someone with my restless nature. Thank goodness, through it all, I kept returning to the hope that I would, *somehow*, achieve my dreams. Something told me to lift my head up and try again—resist accepting the present as the permanent. On many occasions, I felt defeated and spoke words of defeat, but something deep within me gave me the strength to push on. I needed to go places and do things. I had to fulfill my dreams.

In hindsight, I've come to realize that we are all living a dream, whether we realize it or not. The question is, Are you living your dream or someone else's?

One day in 2003, I rode along a bumpy, dusty road in an armored vehicle to the United Nations airstrip in Freetown, Sierra Leone, in West Africa. From there, I would be taking a helicopter to the airport in Lungi to catch a plane to South Africa. I gazed out from the armored vehicle in a hypnotic state at the impoverished people along the dusty road—some missing arms and legs, some with long knife gashes on their faces and bodies, all horrible reminders from the blood diamond war in the region. When we hit a large pothole, I blinked and came back to reality. In a rush to leave the office, I realized that I left a document I needed for my trip on my desk, so I pulled my cell phone out and called my white male subordinate.

"Hey, guess what?" I spoke loud into the cell phone due to the noisy UN helicopters taking off and landing. "I left a brown folder in the center of my desk. Can you please quickly bring it to me at the UN airstrip lounge?"

"Yes, ma'am. I am on my way," a genuinely cooperative voice said on the other end of the phone.

"Please hurry, but ensure the driver proceeds safely," I said. While I wanted the documents, I did not want him to get into an accident, either.

Sitting inside the hot and humid lounge, I was daydreaming of sipping Amarula—a liqueur made from a local African fruit— out of a chilled glass in a plush hotel in South Africa, when I heard heavy footsteps coming my way at a rapid pace. I looked around to see my subordinate briskly walking toward me with an envelope in his hands. I thanked him and was giving him some last-minute instructions when my flight was called for boarding. When I bent down to get my briefcase, he quickly grabbed it before I could get to it. *That was nice,* I thought, as I continued to give him instructions while we walked quickly toward the gate. He was fast, but I was outwalking him because I did not want to miss that flight.

Once we were at the gate, he handed the briefcase to me, tipped his big cowboy hat, and said, "Don't you worry about the office, ma'am. I will take care of it while you are away."

It hit me then—this was the dream from my childhood. No, it was better than my dream. It was the white man hastily walking through the airport, receiving last-minute instructions while trying to keep up with me—the black female boss from Holmestown, Georgia!

I dreamed I was important, and I became important.
I dreamed I mattered, and I became somebody, despite it all.
I dreamed I would travel, and I soared in big planes against
blue skies all around the world.
I dreamed then, now, and until I can dream no more.

Writing poems has always been like an extension of my dreams and a way to express myself when I did not necessarily need an answer but simply wanted to describe what I was feeling or dealing with at that moment in time. When I was just a little girl, I wrote poems under the big oak tree because I knew there was something bigger and better than Holmestown. While I was in college, I wrote poems to keep me motivated to complete my studies in order to realize my dreams. When I was in two horrible marriages, I wrote poems to keep me from doing something awful to those men and to myself. When I joined the Foreign Service, I was basically without family, except for Andrew, so I wrote poems about the innermost feelings of my heart. Writing poetry was my therapy when I could find no one I could trust to vent to. I didn't write hundreds of poems, just enough to get me through and over things in my life.

CHAPTER 2

Risk

I won some, I lost some!

Family, career, reputation, love, safety—of all the things I value in the world, these are some that mean the most to me. To lose one of these would be to lose a part of me. Yet I'm not the type to hold on, dreading the unknown and staying stagnant because of the uncertainty of change.

Rather, it's in my spirit to toss the dice and take a risk.

Some people might ask: Why risk following a dream to work in foreign countries? You had a good government job right near home.

The excitement of it, I thought.

Why send your only child to a boarding school when he is already in a school in the country you are in?

I want him to be independent and well-educated, I thought.

You have been married twice; why take a chance on another man with nothing tangible to offer, not even a car, when you are surrounded by men of wealth with so much to offer?

This one could be the One, I prayed.

For God's sake, you walked out of a bombed embassy facility! Why would you risk your life again and again by going to countries known to be dangerous? *Because it is exciting, and I am an adrenaline junkie. I perform best in crisis mode. I like the excitement. I am alive when living on the edge.*

It took years to move through the bureaucracy of the application process before I was offered a position in the Foreign Service, and there was no rhyme or reason to the timing or sequence of correspondences. A request would arrive for a phone number of someone I used as a reference or for a college transcript; I would compile the information and send it out into the black hole I called my mailbox. Months would go by. I would forget I had even applied. Then, without warning, an envelope would appear, tucked between bills and fliers, asking me for something else. At times, I doubted the job existed. *Somebody's just jerking me around,* I thought.

The call offering me a position came in the same unexpected way. No matter. Saying "yes" without hesitation had nothing to do with the job and everything to do with my situation. I was out of all viable options to succeed in life that depressing morning. I could use a fresh start. Plus, the lady in the human resources department who extended the offer said they would pay my way to DC, put me up in a nice hotel with a spending allowance, and provide free job-specific training. I packed up, dropped Andrew off to Momma until I could come back for him, gave away my mobile home and anything that wouldn't fit in the car, and drove north.

Those first weeks in class were exhilarating. My classmates—all men—seemed smart and accomplished. They were well-spoken and well-dressed. They were overwhelmingly white. I was a minority three times over: black, Southern, and female. *Fine with me.* I was in Washington, DC. The city emanated power and prestige in the same way the heat radiated from the endless concrete sidewalks I saw. I could smell the money, the power.

So, I got the job, but I forgot to do my research and read the fine print. I assumed I would be working in Washington, DC. It was the first of many naive presumptions I would make throughout my career. I had no idea where, why, and what working for the Foreign Service really meant. I had sent various documents to a Washington address. When classmates began talking of overseas assignments, I was flabbergasted, then giddy. While colleagues pursued exotic posts of assignment like Athens, Dubai, Brasilia, Hong Kong, Pretoria, and Montreal, I placed bids for places I knew little about: the Democratic Republic of Congo (DRC), the Philippines, and Honduras, to name a few. I didn't really care where my assignment would be. All the choices were equally foreign and exciting.

Things kept getting better. They provided housing, paid travel expenses to and from the States or another country for rest and recuperation if you were posted to a dangerous or challenging country, and paid for boarding school for my son if schools in a post-of-assignment country were not adequate. They also provided continuing education for me to stay at the top of my field. My gosh, they would even pay overtime for me to dress up and attend official parties and functions where I would mingle with the who's who in the country of assignment.

It became clear that a certain element of danger was involved. We reviewed security regulations and learned how to detect if we were being surveilled. When I called home, I was careful to talk about my training experience in general and use positive terms so my family wouldn't worry, yet I never hesitated myself. Fear is not a natural emotion for me.

In one of the hottest months in 1989, I sat in training, waiting for my name and post of assignment to be called out. When it was called out, it wasn't a true surprise because my Career Development Officer (CDO) had already told me that I wasn't going to get my first choice, the DRC. In that discussion, he talked a lot about the Philippines being ideal for me and my son, since I was separated from Tommie and he was not accompanying us (even though I offered him one last chance to make up while I was in Washington). So when my name was called and "Manila, Philippines," followed, I acted excited, but deep in my heart, I was a little disappointed. I had wanted to go to Africa, the heart of Africa—Kinshasa, DRC. No matter. I was headed to Manila, 8,555 miles away, with my little boy. I had no idea what awaited us, except a job in the US Embassy there.

For the first year, I was wistful about what I had left behind. There was a lot of potential in Georgia. I could have been a big fish in a small pond had I accepted it as what I wanted for the rest of my life. I lost that opportunity, but I gained so much more. As a small fish in a big pond, I had room to grow as big as I wanted. I could do more, see more, and in my career with the Foreign Service, I could advance more. I took the risk, and it paid off big. I went in as a naive backwoods girl and ended up a retired worldly lady.

Risk

By the time I took my next big risk, I was a seasoned diplomat. This time around, risk became personal. Shaka was just a boy in my eyes when I met him in Tanzania in 1997. He was a travel agent whose clients were mostly diplomats. I wasn't looking for a friend let alone a prospective boyfriend or spouse. I only wanted a cheap ticket to a nice vacation spot. I had suitors of all types pursuing me, but I wanted none of them at that time in my life. I was playing hard to get. I did not want any man helping me raise my child—I had enough of that. I had a good thing going on, and I knew it. I was simply waiting for Andrew to finish high school, and then it would be the perfect time to say "yes" to one of those wealthy and good-looking men who were wooing me. Why chance getting distracted from my plans by entertaining the little boy from Tanzania with the big ears and big glasses? I did not need to raise two boys—Andrew and Shaka. So, I saw him and did not see him. I flirted with him, but only so that I could practice perfecting my Swahili and get a better plane seat on a long flight.

Don't go back down that road again, Vella. Don't you give him a second thought, please!

In 1998, I left Tanzania to do a one-year stint in Beirut, Lebanon. I hardly thought about Shaka and his pursuit of me during that time. Then, unexpectedly, we bumped into each other in Arusha, Tanzania, when we were both there on business—he with American Express Travel Services and I was part of a diplomatic visit by the president of the United States (POTUS) that I had volunteered to work. *Hmm, he was a little more refined,* I thought. *Nope, still not for me.* I kept the interactions to a minimum, but we exchanged email addresses the last day of the POTUS trip. I took a second look as he walked away looking disappointed, but I stayed strong. *Not yet, and not this one*, the little voice said in my head.

After weeks of emailing, I found myself gravitating toward him. I liked the conversation—he was quite intelligent for his age. I thought often about how he dressed when we were in Arusha: Stacy Adams shoes and Brooks Brothers suits. I loved his voice. Most of all, I liked the way Tanzanian men acted like they were not really interested in a relationship when they really were. Shaka was no different. He wanted me—and wanted me bad!

Don't do it, Vella. Do not do it.

Six months later, I felt differently about him. I was ready to throw my hat in the ring, and I leaped, albeit cautiously, into a relationship with this man. Yes, he was no longer a little boy. He was grown enough to win my heart, so he was now a *bwana* ("man" in Swahili) in my eyes.

Months went by with me feeling this way and seeing him only once again since our encounter in Arusha. When I realized that I was nearly all in, I declared him to the appropriate embassy personnel as someone of interest to me for a relationship—standard procedures for a US diplomat, especially if you feel the relationship could become something serious and possibly lead to marriage. Shaka felt right, we felt right, and the time felt right. Andrew was in 11th grade with one year to go. I knew I would lose my little boy eventually. I would need someone to fill that anticipated void in my life. This man had the most potential of all whom I had met since I joined the Foreign Service. Aside from that, I felt it was time to get serious, and I came to the realization that wealth was no longer a criterion for a serious relationship. I was back to falling for love, and boy, was I falling for Shaka.

The relationship was moving at a comfortable pace and in the right direction. The stars were lining up for me. About a year later, as I sat on his lap on the balcony of his penthouse in Arusha, gazing at Mount Meru in the brightly lit blue African night sky, I recall thinking, *This is the One I could spend the rest of my life with and be truly happy.* Before I realized the risk I was taking, I was informing the Department of State of my intention to marry Shaka. We did get married, and it was awesome being married to someone who I felt would be a real partner in the marriage, no matter what.

I exhaled as we lay next to each other on the sunny beach of Freeport, in the Bahamas, on the first day of our honeymoon. In my heart, I knew I had made the right decision, but fear creeped into my head. *Do I love him, or do I like him? Does he just want a US visa? Will he leave me to marry who his mother wants him to marry? Can he change that African accent so he can fit into my diplomatic world? Oh Lord, help me please. What have I done again?*

I remember the Bob Marley song that was blasting on the resort sound system at that exact moment I was panicking: "Don't worry about a thing, 'cause every little thing gonna be all right." It was as if God was singing it directly to me. It put me at ease, and coincidentally, it has become our theme song upon arrivals and departures from vacations and when we are facing difficult times in our life. I highly suggest everyone get a theme song to combat worries and stress—it eases tension and clears the head for logical thinking to deal with issues. If I had not heard that song that very moment in the sand with Shaka and decided it would be my medicine to ease my tension, I would have started strategizing my exit out of the marriage without even giving it a fair chance.

The first two years of the marriage were rough, mostly due to circumstances beyond our control. But then God whispered to me via my father: "He is the One; keep this one." This is what my father said to me after he had spent some time with Shaka. Now, 18 years later, I am still happily married and even more deeply in love with Shaka than ever before. I took a chance on leaving what seemed like a perfect "player's life" and followed something that seemed like true love. Guess what? It was true love and still is . . . and I pray it always will be. I won that game of chance—won big!

I have dedication to duty that made me take risks that others may think twice about. I survived the bombing of our embassy in Dar es Salaam. Yet it wasn't enough to risk my life by staying in the building and not immediately evacuating, even after hearing the announcement over the public broadcast system and the wailing sirens in the background. Not me: I had to ensure my office was sanitized and my equipment and systems were properly shut down. Oh, and I had to go into dangerous sections to see if anyone needed help.

This is what I have been trained to do, I thought frantically as I went around securing everything in the office. What I do not recall is being trained to put my life on the line, but I did. What followed later that day and over the next few days made me realize that I risked my life for my career. What did I gain, and what did I lose from these efforts?

Going in and out of a structurally dubious building, most of the time alone, to sanitize or salvage things to set up at an off-site location for operations was dangerous. I gained courage, pride, and a sense of accomplishment. The embassy needed me. The State Department needed me. My staff needed me. My colleagues needed me. I could have asked to be medevacked like some of my colleagues did; I could have mentally and emotionally shut down, but I knew that wouldn't help the horrible situation or my career. I am Foreign Service, and sometimes we do what we must do. It was heroic but suicidal, as my friends and colleagues told me later. I do not advocate anyone putting their life on the line as I did, but you know what? I can't say for certain that I, personally, won't do it again if put in a similar situation. I took a risk on my life when it mattered most. It felt right and good!

Taking a risk is a gamble. I gambled that if my son went to boarding school, he would come out refined, independent and on the road to success. It did not turn out quite as I planned, even though it is still a plan in progress many years later. He went in as my enthusiastic, sharp young boy and came out a stranger to me who spent the next 10 years of his life searching for something. While on that journey, he landed in rehab, two correctional facilities, and one meaningless job after another. I tried my hardest as a mom to fix his problems with money and time, and a lot of "I love yous," but he got deeper into himself and acted out. It darn near killed me to watch him and his life deteriorate, but I always prayed, and still do, that he realizes that I only want the best for him. I took a risk with something I highly valued, and I feel that I lost. Thank goodness, I still hold God accountable for that risk to pay off eventually. I know he will deliver because he has never failed me. It is just taking Andrew a while longer to get his bearings so that he can handle the enormous blessing of success coming to him.

The pain of seeing my son struggle has eased through the years, but not before there was a close bout between Andrew and Shaka that could have been a tragic incident for the family. During the heat of the moment between the two, I cried out, "Please God, please God," and within a minute, the dangerously fiery situation had been doused with tears of hope. A few hours after both of them were calm and talking rationally, I slipped away into the closet of the Washington, DC, hotel suite where we were staying at the time and cried out from the depths of my soul, "God, oh God, help my son right now; help me and Shaka to be able to help him. With your healing hands, please touch this and future situations that may arise until he passes this phase of his life." With that plea, I let God take the reins for my boy's life. *He is yours, God! Use him as you see fit. Please keep him alive for many years, make him good at what he does, and ensure that it is always something positive, and remind him to sing your praises each time he gets another blessing from you.* I can't say that I did not meddle in God's business from time to time, trying to fix things. When I meddled, it backfired most of the time. "Keep your hands off him; you are not the fixer—I am," is what I thought God was saying to me when things backfired because of my meddling. Andrew inched forward with hope when I left things alone and prayed for him.

Andrew is getting his life back on track now, but the damage and pain, not just for him but for those who love him the most, are taking a while to diminish. It will happen, but at God's pace, because I turned Andrew over to him in a desperate, dark moment in his life and mine.

There came a time when I had to decide whether to retire when I felt it was time or when the law mandated it. Talking about the ultimate risk, I just did not know what to do for a while.

Do I stay in until I am forced out at age 65?
Do I stay in until I reach the Senior Foreign Service?
Do I leave when I feel it is time to move on from the Foreign Service?

I was growing mentally and physically tired. It was no longer fun. The work was no longer challenging. I wasn't sure if I wanted to do something different but still within the Foreign Service. Shaka was now in the Foreign Service too, and the separations from serving in different countries were difficult. At one point, we lived apart for three long years prior to us doing a tandem assignment in Afghanistan.

I was tired. But . . . *should I stay, or should I go?* One day, it just came to me clear as day: *I should go.*

As I made my final plans to retire, Shaka struggled to gain tenure in the Foreign Service. Not knowing whether he would continue to have a job strained my planning, but, ultimately, I took a leap of faith (maybe a risk) and decided to retire amid the uncertainty of his career.

"Let the chips fall where they may." I said to myself on my first day back in Washington, DC, to begin the final phase of preparing for retirement. That day I strutted happily down the hall of the Department of State to visit my retirement counselor to discuss my retirement papers. *Tenure or no tenure for Shaka, I am doing this retirement thing,* I thought. *I am not holding on to this career just because. It is time! Leap, girl, leap!*

A month later, the tenure list came out. Shaka's name was on it. He made it! A week after that, the promotion list came out. He was on that list, too. *Wow*! Fortunately, my gamble paid off. I attended the transition seminar the Department of State offered to retiring employees. At the end of that monthlong seminar—which was excellent, by the way—I walked out of the building into retirement with joy in my heart and peace in my life, knowing that the risk I took was in my favor.

One last thing about risk: it is not a risk if there is nothing to lose. I leave you with this incident that happened on the balcony of my house in Tanzania with a suitor who had potential:

"Come close and turn your back to me, Vella." I did it.

"Now, close your eyes." I did it.

"Now, without thinking, fall back into my arms." I did not do it. With eyes opened wide, I turned toward him.

"And if I do not fall?" I asked.

"Then someone else will." He walked away and never looked back.

CHAPTER 3

Perseverance

The tears are uncontrollably
rolling down my cheeks.
My head is pounding
as if a drummer is tapping a tune inside of it.
My body shakes as if I am at the North Pole on its coldest day.
My heart thumps from anxiety
because I don't know what to expect.
I feel so alone.
I called a friend and confidant
only to be greeted by a voice mail.
Oh God, who can I turn to down here on Earth? I have you, I
know, but I need a listening ear down here.
What can I do?
Nothing is going right.
Can this be happening to me?
How can I be so totally helpless?
I want to give up!

Looking back, it's funny how perseverance has played such an important role in my career and life in general. By nature, I am not a patient person.

"You move too fast! You talk too fast! Slow down!" I have heard this from family members all my life.

If I have the information, I make decisions, and if it does not work out, oh well—on to the next thing. It isn't meant to be. It isn't worth it. No need to ponder and wait. That was how I thought in most of my early years in life and in the Foreign Service. I became wiser, slower, and more resolved as time went by. *Slow down and wait, girl; waiting will not kill you.* That is what the little voice in the back of my head says more these days. When it talks, I can feel my heart rate slow down. My nerves calm. My breathing slows. It takes a lot of stubborn body parts to work together to get this ambitious country girl to slow down, but at pivotal points in my life—and increasingly as I grow older—these parts have communicated and made way for perseverance.

When I moved back to Georgia after my first failed marriage, I had no options other than to wait and see how things would end up. I applied to the Foreign Service on a whim, answered the periodic requests for information, and went about my daily life. It was but one of the 50 applications I sent out within a short time frame and promptly forgot about. I didn't know that it would turn into a two-year process that required a whole lot of patience.

As for the Department of State, someone from the human resources department would call occasionally to ask for a little more info. That was my notification (or should I say hope) that the process was still moving forward. I didn't know positions in the Foreign Service were some of the hardest government positions to obtain. My life during those two years was a constant thunderstorm. I forgot about that position, but not my dreams. After about six months of waiting and talking to HR, I realized that it would be a long process, so I told myself, *You can't speed this one up, so just slow down.*

I didn't know at that time that the waiting was sort of a "weeding" process, as I interpreted it later when I had the opportunity to do a short stint in the recruitment office of our HR bureau. If everything else worked out, most of those who didn't give up received offers to join the Foreign Service. They persevered and passed all the assessments, obtained a security clearance and a Class 1 medical clearance, and passed suitability—all very challenging, time-consuming steps in the hiring process that take a toll on your nerves if you aren't patient. Back then, I observed, the majority of those who stuck it out were "white, male, and Yale," as a former senator once said. For me, waiting on the Foreign Service was not just perseverance for a dang awesome career, as was the case for so many of my colleagues. It was perseverance out of ignorance. I didn't have a clue why it was taking so long because, to be perfectly honest, I knew almost nothing back then about the Foreign Service and why those hired had to go through such rigorous screening. Now I know! The first and most important thing I tell those bright-eyed and enthusiastic folks who ask me about the process of joining the Foreign Service is to be patient.

After joining the Foreign Service, my first true experience with perseverance came when the State Department suspended my security clearance after I married Shaka. I knew the risk of marrying a foreign national. It's in the Foreign Affairs Manual and was covered in the written and oral briefing I was given when I informed embassy officials about my intent. However, once I found out that the suspension of my clearance was related to my marriage, I tortured myself trying to figure out how such a great, rule-abiding Foreign Service employee like me could have her security clearance suspended for such a reason. It just did not make sense to me.

Folks liked me. I was now married, with a son in college, respected by everyone, and I knew my job and did it well. I was living in Yaoundé, Cameroon, in 2002, my eighth assignment since joining the Foreign Service in 1989. It was my third assignment on the African continent, and I'd grown to love its people, culture, raw beauty, and even the challenges it brought in performing my duties. Shaka and I were loving it there. Andrew visited several times from boarding school before going off to college. For him, going home on vacations meant going to Africa, since it was where his parents lived and worked. How exotic is that for a black American teenager?

Living and working in Cameroon was perfect. On local holidays, we toured the Cameroon countryside and rainforests, both teeming with exotic animals and plants. Shaka and I threw great parties where our staff would come to our home the morning of the parties to prepare the local dishes. They also taught Shaka and I how to prepare those local dishes we loved the most. This was the perfect way of getting to know our staff and their culture better.

My work was equally satisfying. I enjoyed the challenges and spent countless hours updating standard operating procedures (SOPs) and modernizing the office. The ambassador was friendly and accessible. My staff and colleagues couldn't have been nicer and easier to work with.

One morning, I arrived early to tie up loose ends in preparation for the arrival of our new Deputy Chief of Mission (DCM). My office would be one of his first stops, as I had to give him his computer security briefing and login information. No matter what rank you were in the embassy, my office was one of the first you visited upon arrival. So, when someone knocked at my door, I fully expected to see a new face—the new DCM. Imagine my surprise when I was met by the Regional Security Officer (RSO) holding a piece of paper in his hands.

"Hey, what's up? How can I help you?"

He handed me the sheet of paper in his hands. It was a telegram. I read it, then read it again.

"What is this about?" I asked, feeling faint.

"I don't know. Do you?"

"I have no idea." I whispered because now I was feeling choked up and had to squeeze words from my throat.

The telegram informed me that my security clearance was suspended. I was no longer allowed in controlled areas of the embassy.

Oh God! What was I supposed to do? I thought. *The controlled area is where I perform my duties.*

Horrified, I saw my life pass before me. A knot formed in my stomach when I contemplated my return to Holmestown—again! I could hear my mom say, "You have fallen from sugar to shit again!"

The RSO cleared his throat. The sound of it snapped me back to reality.

He told me to gather my belongings because he had to escort me out of the controlled access area.

How humiliating and scary to hear those words and not know the reason for it. I could no longer be in the controlled areas of the embassy due to my security clearance being suspended, but why? No explanation was on the telegram.

I logged off my computer and got my purse. I notified my American staff next door in the communications center that my security clearance was suspended, so I had to leave the controlled access area. I could not answer their questions as to why or for how long. They looked baffled, especially seeing the dazed look on my face, with the RSO standing inches behind me.

"We'll be in touch when we learn more from Washington," he said, walking me out the front of the controlled area and into the lobby.

I stood in the middle of the lobby for what seemed like eternity. *There must be a mistake,* I thought. I wracked my brain over my comings and goings, conversations I'd had, side trips I had made. Nothing pointed to a reason for having my clearance suspended.

Up to that point in my career, I had known only a handful of people who had their security clearance suspended, and never in my wildest dreams did I think I would be among them. I managed to drive home and call Shaka at his office to tell him that I was home—I did not go into detail about why.

"Are you sick, babe?" he asked.

"No, I will tell you more when you come home."

"Shall I come now?"

"No. Just stay and work," I said.

That afternoon when I picked him up, I was calmer but still extremely worried. We said little on the ride home.

For the next several days, I lived in pure hell, waiting and not knowing.

Finally, tired of being in limbo, I went to the embassy one morning to cash a check and speak to the ambassador. His secretary came down to escort me inside. We said nothing on the elevator ride.

When we got to the ambassador's office, the ambassador, warm as ever, extended his hands.

"Vella, I heard about your clearance issue," he said. "I am looking into it. It caught us by surprise." He empathized with me and asked if I needed anything.

"Sir, with all due respect, I joined the Foreign Service to perform a full array of duties, and if I can't execute all my duties—classified and unclassified—while I am overseas, I need to find out why," I said. "I need answers, and I am not getting them here. I feel isolated, abandoned, and humiliated." I paused, and then went on: "Sir, I believe I should go back to Washington to find out why my clearance was suspended instead of waiting here in limbo. I would like to be curtailed if you would approve it."

He said he would approve it but hated the idea of losing a solid and reliable member of his staff.

True to his word, the ambassador approved the curtailment (cutting my assignment short), and Shaka and I were back in the States within weeks of that day I spoke with him. Thank goodness there was sufficient time for packing up our household effects for shipping back to the United States and for one last farewell get-together with our staff.

It was the grandest farewell I had ever experienced in the Foreign Service. It took place the evening of our departure from Cameroon. We ate and drank sodas. There was some dancing, too. There was also a lot of praying and singing African spiritual songs. I think there were at least five prayers, with one lasting almost 30 minutes. We didn't mind; Shaka and I needed it. Someone was praying when the embassy vehicle entered the compound and pulled up to my door. The male staff would not let us carry our bags. They loaded them in the vehicle for us while still singing.

In the van on the way to the airport, Shaka and I sat there holding hands and smiling at each other, speaking only a few words. To our surprise, when we arrived at the airport, a bunch of our staff who were at the party were there, too. So, there were more goodbyes, singing, and praying. It was so precious and genuine that I felt overwhelmed and started to cry. When Shaka and I finally made it inside the airport and sat down to wait for boarding, we looked at each other and smiled while squeezing each other's hand very tight.

Shaka asked, "What are we going to do now, *mpenzi yangu* (my love)?"

Without hesitation, I responded, "We do not give up."

Hot tears rolled down my cheeks and into my mouth. I felt the salty sweat, and it brought back memories of all the sweating I did in previous assignments on a roof installing radio antennas or outside with local telephone techs supervising cable installations, and when I was in a bombed embassy in over 100-degree temperatures, working when I should not have been. I turned to Shaka and said, "Sweetheart, I do not know why my clearance was suspended, but we will not give up. I have shed blood, sweat, and tears, and did everything by the book for this organization, so I will not give up."

Within no time, we had landed, and I was back on American soil. Being in the States gave me a sense of comfort and familiarity that are lacking when living abroad. I could eat my favorite comfort foods, see my son—who had just started college—more often, and see more of my family and country. It was great. I walked off the plane and felt a burden had been lifted, and that it would be no time before things were cleared up and I would be back overseas at the embassy.

The optimism quickly faded during my first week at the Department of State. I was making little headway in finding out why my clearance was suspended. I had limited access to a computer in the Foreign Service lounge, so I filled some of the working hours emailing friends, but when they found out I had my security clearance suspended, most of them stopped responding. Then, one day, just plain tired of hitting brick walls, I walked out of the Foreign Service lounge feeling defeated. When I exited, I was facing the door of the American Foreign Service Association (AFSA) office. I went through AFSA's door and asked to speak to someone. I was grasping at straws and refused to go on administrative leave to wait it out. So, when the attorney took me to her office and asked me if I was an AFSA member, I thought it was another brick wall. I told her I was not, but I would join if it meant she would listen and try to help me. *Sign me up right now, because I am not quitting.* She smiled and told me that she liked my attitude. She spent the next hour listening to me and taking notes. As I got choked up or sniffled during the conversation, she stopped and let me have my moment. Tears never came, but I had moments that I needed to take deep breaths.

"Have you spoken to anyone in Diplomatic Security?" she asked

I told her I had, but I was given the runaround as to whom I should speak to about the suspension. So, I knew as much then as I knew when I was given the telegram at the embassy in Yaoundé—only that my clearance was suspended.

"So, you were only shown a telegram at the embassy, and nothing else was given to you by the RSO nor have you been contacted by anyone since you have been back in Washington?"

"That's correct," I said.

"Well, then, finding the right office and person for us to speak with about your clearance is the second thing we are going to do."

"What's the first?" I asked.

"We're going to take your dues and sign you up as an AFSA union member."

I felt I finally had someone who cared and could help. As she walked me to the receptionist desk, she told the receptionist to ensure that I joined AFSA before I left the office. She smiled, touched my shoulders, told me not to worry about anything, and walked back to her office.

A few days later, she gave me a number to call to tell them I was coming over to get my information packet. I called right away and was told when to meet a staff member in the lobby of one of the Department of State annexes. On the scheduled date, I was nervously waiting in the lobby when a woman came out of the elevator holding a typical government brown envelope. She stepped into the lobby and started looking around as if she was searching for someone. I walked over to her and asked if she was looking for me—Vella Mbenna.

She looked at my badge. "No, I am waiting for a Vella Wells," she said. At that moment, I did not know how to respond because I wasn't sure if she was being sarcastic or really did not know that Vella Wells was now Vella Mbenna. So, I closed my eyes for a quick second, took a deep breath, and asked God to give me strength and patience. I told her I had gotten married a year ago, my previous name was Vella Wells, and I was waiting to meet a Department of State Diplomatic Security staff member in the lobby. She then asked me a few questions to validate that I was indeed who I said I was. She told me to give her my badge. I did, and she gave me the brown envelope she was holding. I asked her how I was supposed to get back inside any Department of State building without my badge. She told me to look inside the envelope for instructions for getting a restricted badge.

I spent the rest of the morning getting the restricted badge. I felt degraded when I was handed the new badge, but that wasn't nearly as bad as I felt when I was escorted out of the control area of the embassy in Yaoundé. While clipping the badge on, I thought to myself that it was fine for now; at least I still had a job and could fight whatever had caused this from within the department and not while trying to search for a job. I did not read the other documents in the envelope until I got home. I am glad Shaka was not there because I needed time to absorb what was in the document. For confidentiality reasons, I can't share the details here, but suffice to say that I believed I could get my clearance reinstated after finally finding out why it was revoked.

The next day, I gave the document to the AFSA attorney. She was busy at the time, so I returned the following day to discuss it. During our meeting, she told me that her office was seeing an increase in security clearance issues like mine. She said that some staff became frustrated or disenchanted and just quit the Department of State rather than fighting to have their clearance reinstated. Before she went further, I looked her in the eyes and said, "I am not quitting. I am fighting because this is not right." She asked if I could prove my case, and I told her yes. She told me to gather whatever I had to demonstrate that I followed procedures, but not to rush because I was going to be in Washington for a while. I asked her why, and she said that is just how it works.

Over the next few weeks, I looked through emails, notebooks, documents, and files to find the information needed. When I gave the AFSA attorney the last bit of information, she told me that I was an attorney's dream client. I asked her why, and she said that I kept everything, even notes to myself. I smiled. *Martha and Eugene raised no fool.*

"Hold tight. Find an office that does not require a security clearance to work in. We're going to try our best to get you through this, and as painlessly as possible, but it will take time." Patience, perseverance, endurance—you name it, I now had it. I wasn't going anywhere. I loved Holmestown and eventually wanted to move back there after retirement, but there was no way I was going back under these circumstances, especially not without a fight for my career. I did not want to move back home yet; I did not want to disappoint my family, who were now bragging about me, and I did not want to be laughed at again by my friends. Getting my clearance back was about more than my career and livelihood. It was about the image of my entire family and community. I had to prevail. So, I had all the time in the world to sit behind a desk pushing papers. But what I didn't tell the attorney during my numerous meetings with her as we developed my response to the Director General was that the stress was taking a toll on my health, my marriage, and my relationship with my son. My life was hanging by a weak thread.

Shaka had taken a job at Nordstrom at Pentagon City, and with his gregarious personality, he was doing quite well selling men's apparel to the bigwigs in the metro area. He was also studying to take his citizenship test, and I gladly tutored him through civics and US history. But our relationship was rocky due to my sudden mood swings caused by frustration. Every once in a while, I became anxious and wanted my life fixed—and quickly—but I couldn't do anything about the situation, and it manifested in mood swings until I got myself under control to persevere a little while longer. This situation was pivotal, and I had no choice but to weather it. Still, I was human and had episodes that my new husband and dear son had to endure. After

I came to my senses, I always felt so sorry about my outbursts or withdrawals. I believe that both hold it against me even to this day, but I forgive them because they could not understand what their wife and mother—the main breadwinner at the time—was going through. I decided to remain employed by the Department of State and be humiliated and fight for my clearance to make a better life for them both.

I also endured emotional and physical episodes they were not aware of. Andrew and Shaka never knew about my crying episodes when they were not around. And the dizzy spells I frequently had—oh my God, they did not have a clue about them. I made sure that when I felt one coming on, I sat down or held on to something without letting them know what I was experiencing. Those men of mine could not have known the pain and suffering I endured day in and day out. Thus, I forgive them for calling me *mean* and *selfish*.

My lifelong friend Heather, who was still back in Liberty County, Georgia, was one of a few people who I maintained contact with through the years, yet I did not share this dark period in my life with her. I tried reaching out to her for comfort without telling her what I was going through. But she always had cheerful and positive things going on in her life, and there was no way I was going to bring her down with my issues. So, unfortunately, she was not the confidant I needed at the time, yet she would give me moments of distraction during our conversations due to our lifelong relationship. I thank her for that, because every little bit helped.

I could not tell my family how close I was to being out of the Foreign Service. That ate at me, too. Only Shaka and I knew. He and I kept the secret and used code words and gestures to respond consistently when our family and friends asked how we liked the new assignment in the States and why we did not stay long in Cameroon.

"It's fabulous," we'd answer. "We love working in Washington."

"The assignment to Cameroon was reduced to only a year because they needed me to come back to work here—you know, the need of the Foreign Service!"

On the inside, however, we were in pain and fearful. It was tough, rough, and scary.

Andrew and I were also at odds. Ever since he left for college, he did not look or behave like the Andrew I raised and loved, and on top of that, I never saw any grades. I had such high hopes for him. He had been given every opportunity to thrive. Why was he floundering? Only later, when his conduct got out of hand, did I learn, brokenhearted, that he had been using marijuana and drinking excessively. Was it because he knew something bad was happening in my life and I did not share it with him? Did he sense I did not care about him since I married Shaka? Or was it because he was sheltered all his life until this newfound freedom in college gave him autonomy to do whatever he felt like doing with his precious life? I did not know at the time, but I knew what I saw happening to him added to my pain and fear, and I did not know how to help him or myself. I would tell him that what he was doing was wrong, tell him how to do the right thing, and even tell him the consequences of his behavior if he did not change. I saw no change for good. I tried to gain strength to approach him in other ways, but the dizzy spells increased, so all I could do was say, "Son, please, please stop it." He would deny doing anything wrong, but his behavior told a different story.

Shaka stayed far back from our relationship and only interfered when it became very bad. In my frustration, I used to call Shaka a coward or accuse him of just wanting a visa and not wanting to be a part of the family. It was hard for all of us during that period. I do not want to blame my son's downward spiral on what was happening to me in my job because I know what I signed up for when I joined the Foreign Service. If you are suspected of not following the rules, your clearance could be suspended or revoked. However, I believe that Shaka and I could have been better equipped emotionally to help with Andrew's transition to college if we were not preoccupied trying to clear my name. If we didn't have the distraction of me possibly being unemployed in less than a year, I might have had a clearer mind to see signs of struggles in my child's life and be there to help him work through them. As perceptive and sharp as I was back then, I just did not see the signs; therefore, I had to believe it was God's doing as a part of a bigger plan for my family.

So, with that belief that sometimes helps me through the pain of my son's indiscretions, I am unmoved when I hear comments from family members such as, "You did not raise Andrew right," "You should not have dragged Andrew around the world," or "Andrew took his bad habits from his good-for-nothing father you married." The women in my family are the hardest on me, but little do they know, I raised a fine, intelligent, and confident son, and he is on the path God had laid out before him. I never tell them their comments hurt. I am wise and calculated. I do not need unnecessary confrontation or distraction while Andrew, Shaka, and I climb the mountains God has placed in our lives. I definitely did not inform my family about Andrew's issues back during my security clearance problems because I needed every ounce of strength to concentrate on what was happening to the livelihood of my family and to pay attention to my health.

As if everything I have already mentioned wasn't enough to push me over the edge, my beloved daddy had been diagnosed with lung cancer, and it was worsening around that time. He felt that I was headstrong. We butted heads a few notable times while growing up, but when I joined the Foreign Service, we came to see each other differently. He may have seen a little of himself in me. On numerous occasions, while I was home in between overseas assignments, my daddy would tell me I was a brave girl to be traveling to all those countries overseas. He called me his "traveling girl." I loved when he said that because I felt like he was saying, "That's my baby girl. She made it." Everyone back home was proud of Vella Jane, and that is why there was no way I was going to quit and not fight to get my security clearance reinstated.

So, every chance I got to travel to Georgia from Washington, I did. I needed to hear anything and everything my father (and other family members) told me because I drew strength and courage from them. It was hard seeing my father, a good-looking, tall, light-skinned man, grow more and more fragile. Seeing him sit outside under the tree with his oxygen tank in his wheelchair, talking to his friends who stopped to chat with him, brought tears to my eyes sometimes. It made me start thinking of the good and the not-so-good times I remembered growing up.

One of those memories was a whipping I got from him—thanks Brittany (my sister who is one year older than me). I will never forget that one. It was on a hot, dusty day, and Daddy was sitting outside under the big oak tree drinking plum wine with his friends. Brittany ran to him with me trailing close behind. She blurted out to him that it was my turn to wash the dishes, but I was telling Momma it was not. I knew good and well that it wasn't my turn, so I kept playing. Daddy, wanting to show that he had control of his household, snapped off a twig from the oak tree, grabbed me by one arm, and began thrashing me. I kicked and twirled in the dirt, my little body twisting and turning underneath his tight grip. When Felix Brown, one of his friends under the tree with him that day, had enough of seeing me beaten, he told him that it was enough. Daddy did not listen to him. He kept at it. Crying and screaming, I could see Brittany peeping from behind the oak tree, those big brown eyes of hers clouded with fear that maybe she made a mistake going to Daddy in order to get out of her turn washing the dishes.

He stopped only when my mother came outside and snatched me away.

Funny, I didn't hate him regardless of why I got beaten. However, right after each beating I received from him, I considered him a coward, a bully who felt big by beating us kids. I guess most kids feel that way. Little did I realize that he was being a dad, and if it weren't for those whippings, regardless of who was right or wrong, we would have grown up quite differently and possibly tragically.

When I was a little girl, there were times Daddy wasn't around the house much. He was either working or out with his buddies. He loved moving about, going places. My mother remarked more than once that I shared his restless nature. "You always want to be in the street, just like your daddy. Stay your behind at home," she'd say. I knew she would never allow me to run the streets, but I always asked if I could go to a sports game, to a cousin's or friend's house, or to a party, even if just next door. I tried my luck and took chances because sometimes she would throw a jab at me for bothering her with the foolishness, and sometimes she would let me go. Maybe that is how I grew to be a risk-taker.

Momma did not stop telling me about my restlessness after I became a young adult. "You are your daddy's child, always going somewhere," she said when I was in college and even more when starting my career. She did not know that I loved traveling and wanted to make a career of it. "You are so free until you are a fool," she used to say. That phrase used to hurt me to the core. She really did not understand my passion, and she called me a fool for something she did not understand.

I came to realize that the traits I hated most in my father—his drinking spells and bouts of absence from home—were born from a life boxed in, from a lack of opportunity. In some ways, I believe he was happy that I loved to travel and ended up with a career built around traveling because it was an extension of his passion and love to be "gone."

"My traveling girl," he would say. I know I made him proud.

During the time of my security clearance saga, I made frequent trips to Georgia to visit family, but mostly to see my dad and take him places and buy him things. Deep down, I knew he would leave soon, and I did those kind things for him in an effort to let him know that I forgave him for what I thought he was or was not as a father when I was young. Also, I just wanted to show him that his baby girl made it big. Each time I visited, Daddy grew more gaunt, listless, deflating before my eyes. Each time I said goodbye, I was convinced it would be the last.

Everything happening in my life was bad, and I grew depressed and quiet. I did a lot of reflecting and analyzing. As much as I wanted to overturn my suspension issue and get back to my life,

I wasn't sure if I would survive my personal problems in such a sea of uncertainty. So, I reflected more and analyzed more. I delineated and tried to account for everything happening in my life—bit by bit.

I kept hoping for a miracle. Being a devout Catholic, Shaka found a Catholic church when we first arrived in Washington. It was on the Fort Myer military base. If we were in town on a Sunday, we were there. We prayed and prayed in that church. I sometimes used to wonder if folks could see our pain. It didn't matter. We felt comfort in that church and knew that God was hearing us and would work it out, but in his own time.

I went off to work every day with a smile, fearing I would run into someone who knew I was back in Washington with a clearance issue. Of course, I could not work in the controlled area, so I landed a job in the recruitment office in human resources. One of my past career development officers, who was doing a stint in HR, needed help. When I asked for the job, she gladly took me under her wing. It was awesome. I am not sure how much she knew of my situation, but she never asked.

Soon, she got me out of the office to do a few recruitment assignments at job fairs and universities in the DC-Virginia-Maryland metro area. She told me that I was a natural with people and great at recruiting. She asked if I wanted to do some job fairs alone. I said yes because, to be honest, I loved talking about the Foreign Service. *Ironic,* I thought. *I'm sincerely singing the praises of the Department of State Foreign Service while they have turned my world upside down!*

In March 2003, I opened yet another brown envelope from Diplomatic Security. I knew it was the decision; my gut told me it was. It had been about nine months since I came back to DC seeking answers, so it was about time to hear something. I closed my eyes: *Please God, let this be over. Let me be cleared.*

"Ms. Mbenna, after a review of your files, it has been determined that . . . free to return to work overseas." Those are the only words my brain could comprehend as I read the letter twice. All the other words were insignificant.

I had my career back. I persevered. I prevailed.

I went quickly to the AFSA office to share the good news with the attorney.

"This is awesome news and a rare accomplishment!" she said with a big smile on her face.

She read the letter again before coming from around the desk to hug me. While patting me on the back, she said, "What is rarer is coming across folks having the perseverance and positive attitude you have exhibited to get through such an ordeal."

"You are a tough cookie, Vella. You stuck it out and won. You and Shaka did it. You have your security clearance back and are free to go back overseas."

She hugged me again. Relief washed over me. All I wanted was to get back to work and get my good name back.

I wasted no time putting in bids for overseas positions. Outside the normal bidding window, there were few assignments in coveted places like Europe or South America. However, there were plenty of assignments in my beloved Africa, so I placed my bids and was paneled for Freetown, Sierra Leone.

I am going back to the land of my ancestors. I'm back, I'm back.

History has it that folks from Georgia and South Carolina (and a few other Eastern Shore states) originated on slave boats from Sierra Leone, Liberia, Senegal, and a few other countries in that region of Africa. I was excited about getting assigned to Sierra

Leone, but, ultimately, it did not matter where I was going—I was just thrilled that my clearance was reinstated, and I was going back overseas.

A week before I left, I visited the folks in Georgia to tell them I was going back overseas on a new assignment. Daddy looked stronger than normal one day when we were on that visit home. He asked me and Shaka to take him to Broad Level, a community in Long County where he was born and raised, to visit his family and friends. He did not get out much those days. We were happy to oblige him, so the next day we made it a full day of going from house to house on Broad Level with Dad. He did not even carry his oxygen tank. He really seemed stronger. Late in the afternoon, after he visited everyone he could think of, he showed us a shortcut from Broad Level that he used to take to see my mom in Holmestown. That day was so much fun—I had forgotten that just weeks before, I was depressed and worn down.

Daddy had a full day, so he went to sleep early. The next day, Shaka and I had to leave to go back to Washington to catch our flight to Africa in a few days. Andrew was home from college that weekend to be with us, so we got a chance to give him a hug and say goodbye to him along with the rest of the family.

After putting the suitcases in the car, I went to say my goodbyes to those in the house. I walked past Daddy, who was sitting on the back porch, watching and smiling as we moved in and out of the house with suitcases. As I walked past him, he said, "You better talk to Andrew before you go back overseas." I said I would, thinking he sensed that his grandson might be sad and was going to miss us now that we were headed back out of the country. Then Daddy went on to say, "I think Andrew is smoking."

Baffled, I blinked a few times and swallowed deep before asking him why he thought that. He said that he saw Andrew hiding behind a tree smoking a cigarette earlier that morning. He told me to remind Andrew that smoking will kill him if he doesn't stop. I told him I would, but now that I was going back overseas, I needed Daddy to tell Andrew too. As I turned to walk into the house, I saw Daddy with a sad look on his face. He was looking toward Andrew, who was standing in the yard with his hands in his pockets, appearing eager for us to leave, I guess, so he could return to a life free of his parents and back to his downward spiral. I felt so sorry for my baby boy but figured that now that my life was stable again, I was strong enough to help him. When I returned to the porch to tell Daddy I was leaving, Andrew had moved closer to the porch. I reached down and hugged and kissed Daddy. I looked back at my son and told him to spend the rest of the day talking to his granddaddy before he was picked up to go back to college with his cousin who lived in Atlanta. He eagerly said, "OK."

"I will see you later when I return from overseas, Daddy. Take care of yourself, OK?"

Daddy took my hands and squeezed them. While looking in my eyes (which was rare), he said, "I won't be here when you get back."

I laughed and looked at him with a half frown before I said, "Where are you going to be, ol' man? I will be back in six months or so."

"I will see you on the other side, traveling girl—now go on and be good before you miss your plane."

I knew what he meant but did not accept it. His coloring was good. He was walking around and only used the wheelchair when he wanted to go down the road to get away from Momma's nagging. Every time I left Georgia, I left with the realization that it could be my last time seeing him, but this wasn't it, I thought to myself.

I was wrong. While visiting Shaka's parents in Tanzania before traveling on to Sierra Leone to begin my new assignment, I got the call. Daddy had died. Suddenly, the whole clearance debacle made sense: God needed me stateside to teach me perseverance and to spend time with Daddy before he passed away. In that moment, the true purpose for my suffering due to my security clearance suspension was made as clear as the blue Georgia sky that started this journey.

I could have gotten too big for my britches in the Foreign Service. I could have pushed people too quick and too hard because I was out to excel and wanted those around me to excel at my pace. I could have been as impatient as ever. I had to be slowed down. I needed to know suffering and patience.

As far as the relationship with my daddy, working stateside during his last year on earth was a blessing from God. This would have never happened if I had not been yanked back to Washington, DC, while God worked out my issues. I would not have been able to live with myself knowing that my daddy and I had not bonded like I truly wanted and needed. So, I forgave the system for turning my life upside down. I forgave everyone who shunned me throughout the process. I forgave myself for thinking I wasn't good enough or that I had done something to bring such chaos upon myself. I embraced the idea that everything happens for a reason. It was a path I had to travel—a cross I had to bear. And I embraced something I thought long lost: an inner peace that I hadn't felt in a very long time.

I'd like to tell you that learning how to persevere is a "one and done" deal. Not so. Persevering is a life skill learned many times over. Major life changes are an obvious point for persevering—diplomats move to different countries with different colleagues and languages every one to three years. There are unexpected situations, such as the issue with my clearance. What surprises me is how minor issues can be just as taxing, especially for new diplomats only a few months into their assignments. Things as simple as using public transportation, finding familiar ingredients to make familiar meals, and even learning how to turn on the shower in a new country have sent me over the edge.

Like other jobs, dealing with unbearable colleagues is a true test of perseverance. I thought the Foreign Service would be a hotbed of politically astute, gregarious, people-loving adventurers, and, for the most part, it is. Yet, as in other office environments, one bad apple can spoil the bunch. I dealt with insubordination, racism, sexism, senses of entitlement, and chauvinistic attitudes in various posts of assignment, but nothing prepared me for the situation that pushed me to the edge of a nervous breakdown at one of my assignments.

The perfect Information Management Specialist (IMS) on paper is intelligent, experienced, flexible, capable, and a team player. However, you may get something totally different when you work beside them or, Lord knows, have to supervise them. At one very challenging post, I had to contend with an unreasonable and stubborn IMS—who had a superb résumé. When I would not support a personnel action this person proposed due to lack of documentation, this IMS became extremely difficult to manage. Instantly, I became the enemy—the boss who would not support her staff. That was the beginning of a tough battle trying to supervise this person. Thank goodness, I had only one year remaining at the post of assignment when this situation came up. When I took the issue to management, they attempted to intervene, but this IMS would not cooperate, even with them. For some odd reason, management decided to just back off and let it play out. Letting it play out meant that I had to supervise an unruly employee for over a year. It was nerve-racking, but I now had experience with perseverance. I was not going to give in, and I did not.

The IMS staff member and I were cordial to each other in the office and at events. The staff member came to me with non-work-related issues and sometimes for advice. I made it work. Before long, I had my orders and was preparing for my next assignment. I made it through despite the system again making me endure something that was not necessary and testing my perseverance. At the party my office staff gave me before I departed that assignment, that IMS was there and told me how much I would be missed. After the party, the IMS approached me and gave me a hug while looking very sad.

"You are a strong woman and excellent manager. I wish my management style could be like yours, Vella."

Shocked, I said, "Thank you. It takes practice and a whole lot of patience."

This experience with the IMS tested my mettle. It strengthened my resolve and taught me never to give in and to never change a right to a wrong to make someone happy. I took the long and tough road instead. I accepted that I couldn't change this person or management. I could only allow change in myself—or not. I allowed perseverance to kick in. I left that post of assignment with my head up and my integrity unaltered.

I've realized that persevering in challenging situations comes down to outlook. I've mostly walked on the sunny side of the street. My cup has always been half full.

CHAPTER 4

Resilience

The cornerstone to resilience is the love, trust, and encouragement shown by family.

After the US Embassy in Tanzania was bombed in August 1998, I remember the paralyzing effect it had on some of my colleagues. Sitting in the van to go from the bombed embassy to our safe haven, I saw the traumatized faces of people clenching their seats and holding each other or a wounded area of their body. When we arrived at the safe haven, they huddled inside the house, stunned, some unable to contribute, even though I know they wanted to. I understood their fear. I, too, was shaken by the disaster. Had I stopped to think about the effects of what had just happened, I might not have made it through that day without breaking down. Looking back, I believe I kept my composure by concentrating on getting needed equipment out of the embassy and reestablishing communications.

Yet weeks later, when the reality of a new normal had set in for most of us, it was obvious that what had happened had a deep effect on us all. Folks were just not the same. Some who I thought were slackers had stepped up to the plate and were working like crazy. Some who you would think would be resilient and hard-charging after such a horrific event seemed to have retracted into themselves and sometimes had to be told step-by-step what to do. It was like I had to learn how to work with a new team amid chaos. It was quite an experience, because I was new, too. I never knew I could stand tall through such an unimaginable thing. When I saw others breaking down, I stopped and consoled them, thinking deep down, *Why this person and not me?*

It was only then that I recognized an internal trait that had gotten me through many of the hard times in my life. Momma called it "get up and get it done!" Friends said I was not thinking straight because, for days after the blast, I kept going into a bombed embassy that was not structurally sound to bring things out to ensure colleagues could resume work with familiar and necessary items. I did not pity myself or think of my personal safety. When I got up off the floor in my communications center the day of the bombing, I dusted myself off and got things done— just like Momma taught me. I never stopped unless I was sleeping, and I did not do much of that.

A few of my colleagues accused me of being stoic, since I did not linger in what had happened. I laughed when I heard such comments because they were far from the truth; I was thinking straight and cared deeply for all who were killed or sustained injuries. I was resilient. And, my goodness, there was more work to do than ever—and with a smaller staff. I stepped up to the plate and worked above and beyond what was expected of me because it was my duty and because of what was instilled in me—resilience. I joined the Foreign Service to face challenges, and this was the roughest in my career to date

Of all the traits needed to survive in the Foreign Service, resilience is probably one of the most important. Every two to four years, your life turns topsy-turvy. A new job, country, friends, colleagues, phone number, food, lifestyle, climate, house—everything changes. After a hard day at work, when all you want to do is curl up on the couch and watch your favorite television show, you can't, because television programming changes from country to country. You might not even have your favorite coffee mug or throw, as your household effects take months to arrive from your last post. Even after your pots and pans arrive, it's not like you can cook yourself some comfort food. Try shopping for grits in Beirut or guacamole in Kinshasa.

Resilience means pressing on or over obstacles. All that bad crap that went down with my first two marriages? There's no way I could have embraced the possibilities presented by the Foreign Service if I'd had my arms crossed and fists clenched. No sulking or burying your head in the sand. No pity parties. Make amends. Forgive. Be flexible. Move on. Resilience never looks back.

Don't get me wrong. We all make mistakes. I made the same one twice in my early years. When both of my marriages fell apart, I could have folded my life in on itself and become a victim of my circumstances, forever playing the blame game and growing more hateful by the day. If I had been puffed up with pride, I would never have been able to admit that something was wrong.

My high school classmates saw my life as one in shambles. Even worse, they reveled in seeing my life crumble on full display. It would have been all too easy to shrink in light of the deep embarrassment I felt after returning home with my head between my legs, not once, but more than twice. In spite of it all, I was determined to rise again.

I had been a bright star. I was the one who got out of Holmestown, and not via the military or by being a soldier's spouse. Yet in just a few short years, I found myself behind the counter of Grab-a-Bag convenience store, waiting on the very folks whom I had told were crazy to stick around after graduation. "There is a great big ol' world out there," I used to tell them. Now look at me and where I was—running a cash register down the street from my hometown church. It was hard being resilient when I was depressed, yet I put my happy face on and tried my best.

The only lifeline I had at the time was my family. They constantly reminded me who I really was and what I could achieve. Were they disappointed in me? Hell yes, they were. They were angry at my poor choices—they rubbed my face in them because they knew I could do better. But they never stopped loving and encouraging me.

As much as my mother got on my nerves, she continually told me to stand up, stop pitying myself, and start over, but this time, make better choices. She kept the pressure turned high on me—all the time.

Thank God for the rest of my family because if it were just my mom and I, I would have had an unrecoverable breakdown.

I never told Daddy the minute details of why I was back home. I am sure he used to hear my mom cussing and fussing at me, or he saw me in tears outside talking to whichever brother or sister was available to listen to me. One day, I recall Daddy coming outside near where I was sitting with my head down after a tongue-lashing from Momma. He gently said, "Your momma talks trash, but she makes sense. It's not over yet. Listen to what she says and not how she says it, and you will be all right, OK?"

To be honest, I did not know exactly what he meant. I was so depressed about my life, I felt hopeless no matter what anyone said. But I liked the sound of whatever he was trying to tell me, and it gave me the strength to keep holding on.

My big sister Rachel, who knows almost everything about me, used to talk to me a lot during that time. I know she, too, was disappointed, but I love what she used to tell me about life and how to handle it. It all boiled down to "take out the good parts of what happened, Jane, and let the bad parts go."

My brother Steven used to tell me to get back on the horse and keep riding until I won the race. That's it, keep riding. Yep, that's my bro: a man of few but powerful words.

My other siblings had words of wisdom as well: "Hold on, it gets better," "Learn from this mistake," and "This is life; keep it moving, sis."

All my family members had their own ways of loving me through my setbacks and issues. Lord, God, I thank you for them. I obtained strength from what every one of my family members said, or did not say, to me.

And so, I rose again. At some point, I began regaining the gumption to continue—in spurts—even if it was only by mailing job applications. The number of cover letters and résumés I mailed out far surpassed what anyone could have imagined for someone from Holmestown, Georgia. They flung my hopes out to the far corners of the country, like small rocks catapulted from a slingshot.

I learned this: Resilience can be cultivated. I must have had a seed of it growing inside, but it would have never bloomed—I would have never bloomed—without the fertile ground of security and love provided by my family in their unique ways.

I experienced this time and again throughout my career. When I was having a hard day, calling home made things better. Hearing their voices from so far away was hard, but knowing they loved me and had my back gave me the energy and conviction I needed to move forward.

Resilience also comes from knowing you will make it, no matter what. Unlike some of my colleagues, I didn't spend a lot of time anticipating the living conditions at the next post of assignment or wondering how my new boss would be, even when I was assigned to Afghanistan or another dangerous country. I had survived living in ramshackle conditions in South Georgia—I wasn't afraid of anything any country or continent might throw at me.

In those early years after returning from California, I lived with my little baby in an old trailer down a dirt road, with no running water or electricity, for many months. When it rained and the dirt road was too muddy for my car to drive up to the door, I waded in ankle-deep water, with my baby in my arms, to the wooden front steps of my trailer. I took showers the old-fashioned way, with a bucket, and went to Rachel's or my mother's house to use the bathroom. If it was late, my son and I peed in a bucket and flung it into the woods at sunrise. Too much information, I know, but it was a part of my experience that made me so resilient.

Eventually, I got running water and electricity—and my toilet worked. However, it was hard maintaining my necessary expenses on my little salary. I often needed help and went from family member to family member asking for small loans to pay my bills so my baby boy and I could live decent—not comfortable, just decent. Sad to say about someone with a college degree, isn't it? Yet that was my life. Once, when money ran shorter than the month, I needed $42 by the end of the week to pay my power bill or else my baby and I would be in the dark again. On top of that, my baby boy was sick. I put my pride aside for the millionth time and called my sister Emma, who was more than financially able to lend me the money until I got paid. She refused.

"You made your mistakes. Now you must live with them," she scolded.

I was devastated. I never thought I would hear that. Before she hung up, she went on to tell me that maybe if I asked her husband, Carl, he would lend it to me. Well, that was where I picked up my pride again. She was my sister, an equal partner in her marriage, and I did not feel comfortable asking her husband to lend me money. I told her thank you and hung up the phone.

I eventually approached Rachel. Without saying a word, she walked to her room and came back and handed me a fifty-dollar bill. I felt so ashamed because she always bailed me out during those rough times. She was consistent in her love and giving. To this day, she has never failed me.

In hindsight, Emma's decision not to give me the money that day and Rachel's decision to give it to me both strengthened my resilience. I believe Emma wanted me to take responsibility for my life (at least that is how I interpreted it), while Rachel cushioned the bumps. Without Emma's hard stance, I might have grown complacent and lazy, always looking for a handout. However, without Rachel's helping hands and big heart, maybe I would have sunk to a point of no return, and there's no telling who I would have become—personally and professionally.

I owe my resilience to my family—tough love and empathy gave me solid springs to bounce back and keep moving forward.

A piece of advice I give to those in the Foreign Service with thin skin: if you do not have family—far or near—to be the base for your comeback, please find a support group to serve that purpose. In a faraway land, it helps to be able to turn to someone who loves and understands you, the person, not the diplomat. Having that comfort will help you walk taller and faster in no time.

CHAPTER 5

Work

*A career that made you happy, set you up to perform well and
achieve much, retire on your terms, and be healthy to enjoy
the fruits of your labor worked for you.*

Just two days ago, I was reminded why I endured the good and
the bad of the Foreign Service for almost 30 years. Even though
I am retired and should be at home resting, I volunteered to serve
as an escort for the 2016 African Growth and Opportunity Act
(AGOA) conference hosted at the Department of State. It gave me
a chance to feel like I was back at the embassy working a party
and to brush up on my foreign languages as well.

"Good morning, madam. Please follow me."

"Habari asubuhi mzee, karibu. Nifuate huku tafadhali."

"Bonjour monsieur et madame. De cette façon s'il vous plait."

It was awesome to be back in the mix. I had an African déjà
vu moment as I was waiting for a female delegate from South
Africa to climb out of the sleek black SUV that had just arrived. A
full-figured, formidable-looking light-skinned woman stepped out
in boss-lady African attire to die for. She had a shiny bald head
that reminded me of when I cut my hair short back in the day. It
was as if I were looking in a mirror—and not because I could see

the reflection of me on her shiny bald head. She looked powerful, and she knew it. She was poised, beautiful, and gracious. She made me homesick for Africa and the Foreign Service. I wanted to be Momma Africa again. But most of all, she reminded me of how I took my Holmestown beauty, charm, and values around the world as I served my country.

I can't describe how good I felt when I greeted the Tanzanian delegates in their native tongue of Swahili. Their faces lit up with big, warm smiles as they responded. For a minute, it seemed like I was back in Tanzania working the crowd at one of our annual embassy events where we invited local dignitaries.

When all the delegates were in the building, I struck up a conversation with a young person recently hired at the State Department who had volunteered to work as an escort, just like me. He looked at me strangely when I told him that I was retired. "If you are a retired diplomat, why are you escorting?" he asked in a baffled tone.

For a second, I flashed back to the image of a high-level officer sitting on the dirty floor of the embassy, hot and sweating, after escorting staff for hours. It was during our move from an old embassy facility to a new one. The officer had not only escorted staff but also carried small items from the dusty General Services Office trucks into the various offices in the controlled access area of the shiny new building.

"Even though I'm retired, I see the need to help, so I volunteered," I replied to the young man. "That's how Foreign Service personnel, even retired ones, do things—we pitch in when needed to get the job done." I truly hope he understood, especially since he told me that one day he wanted to join the Foreign Service.

In retirement, I still spend a lot of my time describing life in the Foreign Service to those who want to learn more. Some, I can tell by their line of questions, may not be good fits, while some would be. To all of them, I say, "Why don't you ponder everything I have shared with you about the Foreign Service for a while, then ask yourself, 'Is the Foreign Service right for me, or am I right for the Foreign Service?' Then follow your gut response."

All personality types can join the Foreign Service, but it takes a special person to withstand and enjoy the work and lifestyle—to not only be able to say they served successfully when retirement day comes, but to also walk away with a big proud smile, feeling accomplished. Working in the Foreign Service means sacrifice and flexibility: You may have to work a local election when your best friend is getting married back home. You may have to come to the aid of an American citizen when you are out enjoying dinner with friends. You may have to work out of your area of expertise; for example, if you are an Economic Officer, but the Information Management Officer (IMO) needs help removing equipment from an area during a disaster, you pitch in without hesitation. You may have to move out of your comfort zone and attend a party with a colleague who lives an alternative lifestyle when you haven't yet come to grips with the concept. All of this is the Foreign Service life!

On the other hand, for the right person, the reasons for joining the Foreign Service are limitless. Professionally, being able to manage your own work and pitch in to help others when needed is paramount, especially during crisis events or high-level visits. Notice that I said "needed," not "asked." If you must be asked to help when it is obvious a colleague needs help, more than likely this is not the career for you.

There were times when I was given very little notice to prepare for a high-level visit. The work that went into pulling off one of these events was grueling—and that was on top of my day-to-day responsibilities. Weeks, days, hours, and minutes before, I was frantically running around planning, installing, configuring, testing, supervising, and whatever else it took to ensure reliable communication was available before the principal party—who could be as high up as the president of the United States and his entourage—arrived. I ran myself ragged, and in hindsight, my staff members, who diligently ran with me, probably thought I never ran out of energy—the "Energizer Bunny" is what a colleague once called me. As a team, and with me as the leader, we stayed two steps ahead of the game. We had to! If we dropped the ball or were not prepared in a foreign land, who would be there to pick up the ball?

At times, advance notice of an impending visit or change of plans went something like this:

"Ms. Mbenna, there has been a change. We need 10, not two, satellite phones for the trip up-country with the principal. Oh, and we leave in 15 minutes."

"No problem, sir. We anticipated this and someone from my staff will bring them down to the control room right away."

Or like this: "Who is the IMO?"

"Hi, I am Vella Mbenna, the IMO."

"Nice to meet you, Vella. I need a power adapter for my laptop—mine is flaking out on me; please say you can help me. The principal party leaves in an hour for the summit at the conference center and I am one of the notetakers for the event."

"Do not panic. Please follow me to my computer center and one of my staff members will find a solution for you."

I never prepared for the exact number of things requested for visits. Instead, I was always thinking and preparing for the *what-ifs* and the last-minute *I needs*.

Knowing the complexity of and the high energy required for the job, I have always tried to be truthful in recruiting to ensure that skivers think twice before applying. With so many people revolving in and out of the embassy, there are sometimes temporary gaps in the workflow where no one is specifically assigned. If it impedes your job, well, guess who gets to pick up the slack? You!

It's just the way I saw it in the Foreign Service, at least in my field. No matter what your job description is on paper, in the field you can expect it to extend to "other duties as assigned or needed" to get the work done.

Personally, you can't afford to have a reputation for not being a team player. If your co-workers cannot depend on you at work, some may not be inclined to come to your aid after-hours. When you're living in another country without family support, the embassy community becomes your family. You'll count on them for little favors like car rides to a work function when you can't drive yourself or to keep your pet when you go on vacation. These are the people you'll celebrate your birthday with. They empathize with you when you miss an important event back home. More than anyone, they understand the demands of the job, and they are willing to do whatever is needed to help you out, but there must be a feeling of reciprocity.

Above all, being a skiver could get you in serious trouble. Having a laissez-faire attitude in a dangerous foreign country, whether it's walking to work via the same route every day or eating at the same restaurant at the same time on the same days every week, could jeopardize your safety abroad. You could become a soft target for someone who wants to harm you. If you are instructed to participate in radio checks, it is for a reason. If you are instructed to carry your satellite phone with you to a remote area of the country, it is for a reason. Yes, radio checks may impede on your time, or satellite phones may be too bulky to fit in your pocket or purse, but you know what? If you do not know how to properly use your radio during an emergency or do not have that bulky satellite phone when the vehicle has a flat tire in a remote area and your cell phone is dead, you could regret being a lazybones.

Thankfully, I did not come across many colleagues in the Foreign Service who blatantly did what they wanted to do and did not care about following all the rules or pitching in. When I encountered someone like that, I tried to convince them otherwise. I am not sure if those few, when recruited, were properly informed about these details of the Foreign Service.

Today, I think those who are interested in joining want to know the truth. Will I have to drag pouch bags on the airport tarmac as an economic officer? Could my leave to attend important events back home be denied? What does being "flexible" really mean? Does bigotry exist in the embassy? What are my recourses in the embassy if I am being bullied or discriminated against? Do I really have to attend embassy functions if I do not want to?

People also ask how to succeed in such a unique career, and specifically, they want to know how I succeeded as a minority in the Foreign Service. Regardless of what many Americans think, read, or hear, being a minority does not make it easier being in the Foreign Service. If anything, in the 1990s, being a black woman in the mostly white male environment of the Foreign Service, I had to prove myself time and time again to be equal or far more proficient than my male colleagues, and I had to swallow acts of bigotry toward me and others out of fear of being isolated or terminated. It should not have been that way, but it was. Luckily, before I retired, I began seeing changes. There is still more progress to be made, but at least there is more awareness and more recourse available.

Even so, I chose to learn what I could along the way from all types of colleagues—those who treated me fairly and those who did not. As I bounced around the world in various roles, I watched and listened to everyone, picking up new techniques, new mind-sets, and new experiences that helped me develop in my career and as a human being. My thought was that I worked for a country built on diversity, and I was going to benefit from it.

My role models who were higher up in the Foreign Service shared convictions equal to or similar to mine. Knowing this reaffirmed that I could and would make it to retirement in the Foreign Service with the grade I envisioned. When asked by aspiring colleagues how I coped and succeeded among all the craziness at times, I had a mouthful to share about the skills and values that helped me.

Skill number one is: *Do the work—and more.* My mother drilled into me the importance of waking up early, being prepared, and taking the time to do things right the first time. After that, help others who can use your assistance. I've never known anything different because Momma never gave us the chance to experience what lazy felt like. Every day—and I mean *every* day—we came home from school to hear her rattle off what seemed like hundreds of chores for us to do before the sun set. If one of us got done first, she made us help another sibling. That was my norm back then, and it became the same in my career. So, "other duties as assigned" was fine with me.

Momma's "hard work from dawn to dusk" mandate is a legacy that has been handed down in our family from generation to generation. Working hard and taking your job seriously are important. Thanks to Momma, I was never referred to as a skiver, especially not in the Foreign Service. No sir, not those from the Martha Rae and Eugene bloodline. A host of family craftspeople and professionals are testaments to my momma's mandate.

I took my momma's mandate with me into the Foreign Service. If the embassy working hours were from 8:30 a.m. to 5 p.m., I worked from 6:30 a.m. to 7 p.m.

I felt it was necessary to arrive a couple of hours early to ensure all the systems I was responsible for were up and running so that my customers—my colleagues—could sit down and start work immediately. If there was a computer system failure, I wanted to know so I could get it resolved or get a team member in earlier to fix it before everyone got to work, especially the Chief of Mission and his deputy. There is nothing as daunting as having the office manager from the executive office—or one of the executive officers themselves—call you at 8:05 a.m. to say:

"The ambassador can't log on—come now!"

Or:

"Good morning, Vella. This is the ambassador. I came in early to make a secure call to the Secretary of State, and my secure phone is dead."

One of the biggest eye-openers I had in the Foreign Service was how someone could sit by during a time of calamity and not lift a hand to help. I saw this firsthand during the aftermath of the bombing of the embassy in Dar es Salaam, and I wasn't quite sure how to handle it. At one point, I was trying to put up an antenna myself, but it was obvious I needed help. One of my colleagues was standing by, looking bored. *Was this person shell-shocked or being a skiver?* I thought as I sneaked a peek in that direction.

The bombing of the embassy scared everyone, but this was a tragedy, and we needed every able body we could get to help set up things at the safe haven. But some just stood by and never asked if they could help. I wanted to get mad and say something, but I was wise enough to not say a word. Instead, I kept doing what my momma taught me. I worked doubly hard. It was worth it because I felt accomplished after the crunch period subsided. Months later, when I received a Heroism Award for my actions during that horrific event, I knew it was well-deserved. Momma's mandate paid off!

Skill number two is: *Find a role model/mentor.* Many years ago, at Fort Stewart military base in Hinesville, Georgia, I was in management overseeing data collection and report writing for rightsizing the workforce. Over time, I noticed that more complicated work was being sent my way. I did not complain. My momma had prepared me for this. My team lead (and now one of my oldest and dearest friends) evidently saw potential in me and kept piling on the work. Years later, she told me that my inquisitiveness, eagerness, efficiency, and thoroughness were so refreshing that she secretly took me under her wing to develop me. She cleverly passed along complex tasks outside my work requirements to challenge me.

She quizzed me: What if we enter the data a different way on the spreadsheet? What if we changed the report format? Why do you think this position is excess and not that one? Can the work be done with one less staff member? She told me I was smart, that I'd go places. I didn't know it at the time, but she was my first unofficial mentor. At the time, I thought she just wanted to get the most out of me to benefit her team.

The Department of State has a formal mentor program that too many, in my opinion, do not use to the fullest. I do not recall whether a formal program existed when I joined, but early on, I knew that I needed to be beneath someone's wing. Mr. Sparker was one of my first informal mentors.

I recall one day on my first assignment in the Foreign Service abroad—in Manila, Philippines—I was thrown into a high-profile project that I thought I could not handle. It was during the onset of the first campaign in Iraq, and all US embassies were on alert, even in the Philippines. There was no time for mistakes. I went home shaking in fear and cried silently on the edge of my bed. I was sobbing so much I did not hear my son enter the room. I recall feeling his tiny arms on my shoulder and hearing his little voice ask, "What's wrong, Momma? Why are you crying?" I wiped the tears from my eyes and told him, the only person I trusted back then—a 6-year-old, that I was not sure I could do something my boss wanted me to do, and because of it, I might lose my job. This little boy, who I still go to when I need an honest opinion or advice, hugged me and gave me sound words of wisdom. "Momma, you can do it, so stop crying." I told him that I wasn't sure. He then said, "Momma, ask Mr. Ryan for help." I took a 6-year-old kid's suggestion and asked my colleague for help. Mr. Ryan was glad to guide me. He became one of my few trusted friends and my "go-to" person during my Foreign Service career.

From that experience, I did my best to take advantage of the few opportunities to develop trusting relationships with colleagues, in my field or not, whom I could benefit from. Those individuals, some who have passed on, will forever be a part of my Foreign Service experience and success. Mentorship works!

Skill number three is: *Don't be afraid to share ideas.* Do not sit around the table with colleagues thinking you are too low in rank or too ignorant of the subject matter to contribute. You would not be around the table if the organizer of the meeting did not feel you had something to contribute. Meetings are the time for discussing ideas; come prepared with at least one or two ideas or questions, and then communicate them. Around mid-career and tired of feeling stupid sitting in meetings and rarely contributing, my motto became: "If you think it, share it." Unfortunately, by then, I had missed many opportunities to contribute my expertise. I can't tell you how many times I was afraid to share an idea while someone else spoke up and said what I wanted to say. They got the glory, and I got to call myself stupid for not sharing it first.

Skill number four is: *Respect the chain of command.* I am big on this. No leader wants to be second-guessed or challenged by a subordinate, especially not in public. The leader is the leader for a reason. Through the years, I came to realize that I worked better with former or active-duty military colleagues. Maybe it has something to do with my mother being so authoritative, or maybe it was because I lived and worked on several military bases where I was exposed to their effective use of the chain of command, but I respected the chain and I insisted upon respect when I led.

In the wake of the Dar es Salaam bombing, several male colleagues from various countries were sent to assist my team in setting up alternate communications. They were not supposed to take over my operation. One day, I heard one of them stepping out of his bounds by advising a senior-level officer of something he did not have on-the-ground knowledge of without consulting me first. I quickly pulled him aside and reminded him that I was in charge and he needed to vet issues concerning that topic with me, the Chief of Communications, first. He apologized, and all was well henceforth.

On another occasion at another embassy, on the eve of moving from an old embassy compound to a new one, the folks in Washington, DC, sent a temporary person to assist my team due to the complexity of the move and the limited number of people in my office. After a terse introduction, this person went to my second-in-command and told him that he would be taking over from that point onward and my second-in-command should just maintain the office while he coordinated the move to the new compound. Then, he came to me and told me that he was taking the lead in the moving project. In other words, my staff and I should follow his lead. *Did I hear him correctly?* I thought to myself while slightly tilting my head in surprise.

I smiled. Looking him sternly in the eyes without blinking, I said, "You may want to catch the plane you just got off before it leaves, because you have the wrong post."

He stuttered for a second as he regrouped—apparently, he got my message. Then he said, "Well, just let me know what I can do. I am here to help you guys." Now that was the attitude he should have had initially. I was in charge, and I had a second-in-command. He needed to follow our lead. He did, and all went very well. We even became good friends over the years. I think he learned that overstepping boundaries without asking, especially if it is not your project or post, makes for a rough ride and a stressful work environment.

Skill number five is: *Be strategic.* Every job I had was a stepping stone to the next one. I looked for ways to learn skills I didn't have so that I could broaden my expertise. That way, I would be qualified for different positions. Due to this way of thinking and planning, I served in one position out of my original area of expertise. And at a different point in my career, I was offered another position, which I did not pursue for various reasons.

Skill number six is: *Know when to be a leader and when to be a follower.* The higher up I climbed in the Foreign Service, the more leadership responsibilities I had. I was enjoying it. Going to Kabul, Afghanistan, on a hardship tour changed that. That job was out of my professional comfort zone. It was not a leadership role, and I went in knowing I was going to be a follower. Under the circumstances, I became a good one. Nevertheless, I knew that my contribution in whatever capacity I was serving was paramount to the mission's goal, and I was fine with that.

Life at the embassy in Kabul was like living in a fishbowl. We worked, lived, exercised, and socialized on a small compound that looked like a maximum-security prison. The only time I ventured out, aside from going to the airport to fly out of the country, was when I went to Bagram Air Base on a helicopter. It was quite an experience, one that made me long for my fishbowl back in Kabul. I never minded being a peon in Kabul after that: *Copy this for me. Reformat this document. Take notes for me at this meeting.* I was told what to do, and I did it as prescribed with a smile. Eventually, I could see where my contribution was making a difference. Whether you're a follower or a leader, your work counts. Whatever role you find yourself in, it matters, so why not make it work for you?

Skill number seven is: *Be dedicated/be useful, even in bad conditions.* Do more than your specific duties—pitch in and help others, even if they do not ask. If they do not need your help, they will tell you. It's called *going the extra mile.* I learned what this meant during my last Foreign Service assignment in Tunis, Tunisia. It was several years after the Arab Spring, in which a series of anti-government protests, uprisings, and armed rebellions were successful in ousting the standing president at the time in that country. Turmoil had resulted in staff reduction and a revolving door of temporary staff at the embassy to try to return operations to normal status. Finally, permanent staff were returning to fill positions, and I was one of them.

During my first meeting with the ambassador upon my arrival, he had several major projects for me to complete during my assignment. One was to prepare for the Office of Inspector General's inspection of embassy operations. The inspection was due within six months of my arrival in the country, so I jumped in with both feet. However, two months after that meeting, there was a leak in my house, and I slipped and broke one of my legs. I was laid up in a hotel room for about six weeks while my house was being worked on. I could have insisted on going back to the US to heal and enjoyed a long vacation, but that was not me. I stayed in country and did as much work over the phone or with staff visiting me as I could while I was healing in a hotel room in Tunis.

Never once did I let up on my responsibilities, but it was draining. One night, after tossing and turning, feeling sorry for myself, and not knowing why this was happening to me, I had an epiphany: This was my cue that it was time for me to leave the Foreign Service—retire. Which brings me to my last skill that served me well in the Foreign Service.

Skill number eight is: *Know when to leave.* The minute I had my epiphany about retiring, I felt a sense of peace and calmness come over me. I was eligible at least four years earlier. Why in the heck did I stay in so long after I was eligible to retire?

The answer? I loved my job. I loved traveling. I loved working with such interesting people. And I loved doing something I believed in. But it was time to move on. On my first day physically back at the embassy, I hopped on my crutches to my supervisor's office to announce my retirement. He laughed. "You can't retire, Vella. You're too young. You can't cut your tour short." A lot of doubt and disbelief is all I heard until I walked out of the embassy nine months later in mid-August 2015 to catch my flight to Washington, DC, to start finalizing my retirement. Before departing Tunisia, I received my flag from the marines to commemorate that it was my last official assignment overseas as a US diplomat prior to retiring. I was proud, accomplished, and teary-eyed. I was going home alive and in one piece, without being forced out or disgruntled, and at the tender age of 54, soon to be 55 a month and two weeks before my official retirement date.

I loved my career, served my government well, and had fun doing it. Who would cut such a great gig short for no good reason when they could work 10 more years before reaching the age of mandatory retirement? I had no concrete plan for what came next, but I had some ideas: babysit my three wonderful grandkids, attend to my aging mother, write a book, get a fun part-time gig, be the housewife I have always wanted to be, or just flounder around doing whatever crossed my path for however long I wanted to. I only knew it was time to retire, and I did it on my terms.

CHAPTER 6

Identity

When I embrace who I am, I rise!

It took a few years after joining the Foreign Service for me to open my mouth in meetings. That's right—ebullient, outspoken Vella, *afraid* to give my opinion for fear of sounding ignorant or Southern. I was not groomed for this path, even though I dreamed of it from a child.

I didn't start out that way.

During my training in Washington, I was so proud to have been selected. It tickled me to say that I was a US diplomat in my Southern accent, and I made a point to say it as often as possible. I'd let it slip when making small talk with the cashier at the grocery store. If a waitress asked what business brought me to town, I'd smile. "I'm in the Foreign Service," I'd say, straightening the napkin on my lap.

My favorite memory entails presenting my diplomatic passport as a form of identification at the airport in Riceville, Georgia, after visiting family that weekend in Holmestown. The airline clerk, a white female, asked for a second form of identification.

"Why?" I asked.

She leaned over and consulted with her colleague, a white male. They looked at me; I smiled back, my nose so high that if it had rained, I would have drowned. It was a legal form of ID, not often found or used, but because of it, I knew they had nothing on me. She handed it back and checked me in. I have no idea, to this day, what that was about.

Many of my classmates exuded the same kind of pride, and, at first, I didn't realize that most of them had studied foreign policy, history, political science, or international affairs, intent on pursuing life as a diplomat or public official. They appeared smart and well-educated, with degrees from universities I only dreamed of attending, not that I couldn't if I had the knowledge and funds to get in back then. I pinched myself to make sure I was one of them, little ol' me, from Holmestown, Georgia, who graduated from Georgia Southern College with my Bachelor of Business Administration degree. In a class picture we took, I am beaming at the camera, a black island in a sea of white, smiling proudly—the only female and the only black person.

Still, having returned home twice thinking I had made it, I told myself that even though I was among the elite, I would never lose sense of who I am and where I was from. I was proud to be from Holmestown, even now. I recall a discussion that I once had with colleagues about our favorite vacation spots, and the response that came out of my mouth was shocking. Broad Level—somewhere just as isolated as Holmestown—is what I told the group. It is where my father was born and raised. As a child, going there was going on vacation, and every time I think of it, even today, I feel a sense of calmness and relaxation. We would jump in the back of a green pickup truck that belonged to Rachel and her husband, Adam, and start singing songs as the wind blew through our hair on the way to Granddaddy and Grandmomma's house. Broad Level, Holmestown, and all the relatives from those locations shaped me. I am Holmestown. I am Broad Level. I took those places and people with me in my heart around the world.

When I gave my response and the short explanation, I could see baffled faces. They all named exotic places around the world, many of which I had lived in or visited. Yes, indeed, I had also traveled the world and taken vacations in exotic places, but every time, returning home was the best place ever to vacation. It is where my roots are, and while others like to run barefoot on the beaches of Valletta, Malta or Cancún, Mexico, I like to walk barefoot on the land of my parents, whether it's in Holmestown or Broad Level. Touching that land with my feet is like reaching back over 100 years to the days when my grandparents' grandparents were sharecroppers. That is what I ended on when I shared that my favorite vacation spot was Broad Level. Broad Level and Holmestown keep me grounded, as I sometimes get caught up with people and places that have nothing to do with who I really am, and I need that jolt of reality—that jolt of identity.

In my initial training with the Foreign Service, I found myself intimidated and unsure of myself as we delved deeper into the courses and seminars. I grew quiet after a while. Before my arrival in Washington, DC, I could have been mistaken for a Georgia elitist—after all, I might have grown up in Holmestown, but I was a college graduate with a government job. Yet in Washington, I arrived green. I had a Southern accent. I was the only black person in most of the classes I took at our training center. I was the only woman in even more of them. Honestly speaking, sometimes I would look around and, when I realized I was the only black or female there, I would get scared. Of what, I do not know, but I did.

I had almost no idea about the role the Foreign Service played on the world's stage, and the learning curve was severe. I was not going to be a reporting officer, but I had to support their official role and socialize with them outside of the office. So, I needed to know what was going on, and it was hard playing catch-up, but I did it. The communications coursework wasn't that easy, either. I spent my nights reviewing the next day's classwork so I could at least follow the discussion. It wasn't that I didn't understand the lectures; it was as if I had simply arrived in the middle of a conversation with none of the backstory that put current events and procedures into context. We had lectures on high-level processes like information security and why it was important in that day and age, and my classmates contributed vigorously to the conversation. They knew about those things. I was fresh, but I also knew I was smart. I had to think fast and research deep to keep up with them, and I did. By the time training was over, I knew as much as they did, but I sure didn't feel that way.

In Manila, my first post, my fellow diplomats cut me some slack for my naiveté. My white male colleagues took me under their wings and guided me through both elementary and advanced processes in my role as Support Communications Officer (SCO). I was blessed and highly favored, I thought, as they used to compete to see who would school the new black girl.

The first time I processed live telegraphic information, my favorite colleague, who became like a big brother to me, demonstrated exactly how to send telegrams, in slow motion. He was patient. I was a nervous wreck. Around that time, tension was escalating toward the first war in Iraq, and information was critical. I didn't want to mess up. As my hands shook, this wonderful man sat behind me, saying in a low, even voice, "You are doing just fine, Vella. Keep going, pick up the pace. I am not going to let you make a mistake. You will be able to do this by yourself when we are done today." He became one of my first mentors before I really knew the full scope of a mentor. We kept in touch until he retired and drifted away into the ether.

Those first few months of my first assignment, I'd go home drained, having poured myself into learning everything I could about the job while trying to be me: Vella from Holmestown. I dared not ask too many questions. Throughout my daily routine, it was as if I were someone else, a voyeur watching the shell of my body go through the motions. On the outside, I projected a pleasant, amiable persona, but inside, I was a nervous wreck trying to absorb it all—the work as well as the new lifestyle of being a US diplomat. I felt myself, Vella from Georgia, drifting away. I was becoming someone else, and, in the process, I felt like I was accepted by the sea of white people around me. I worried that I'd be found out for the impostor I thought I was. It was a tug of war: Am I accepted? Am I right for this job? Where is Vella Jane from Holmestown? I was a total wreck inside.

Why did I feel so insignificant? Why couldn't I speak up when I knew I would be correct? Why at times did I feel like I didn't belong? It was a new feeling, really. Never had I suffered from a lack of confidence, from the idea that I wasn't good enough, from feeling that I could not be myself.

In Peru, my next post, the Department of State decided to change the titles of those in the field. We had to apply for and compete for the new position title of Information Management Specialist (IMS). Later, everyone else was grandfathered in. I had no intention of waiting to find out if that would happen for me. I applied immediately and made it. *Wow*. With the title came a new round of tenure, but I wasn't concerned. I was tenured for the original position title on the first go-round, and I was confident I would do the same for IMS tenure—and I was.

One day, after a full year as an IMS, I was in a meeting with my boss and two American colleagues. When my female counterpart spoke up, I carefully challenged the logic of her argument. They all agreed. *All of them*. Almost instantly, a weight lifted from my shoulders. I had something to contribute, and it was accepted. I did it. The silence was broken. I was an equal in the room, where my opinions were valued and appreciated. I had earned my place at the table. I felt like spilling out every opinion I had squelched over that year—all at once. I finally realized I had a voice that was heard, and I knew countless opportunities were ahead. I felt that I was back to normal; I could speak when and how I wanted to. I wasn't back in Holmestown, but that inner girl from Holmestown was found. I embraced it right then and throughout my career afterwards.

That's a long way of saying that finally, after several years of self-doubt, I remembered who I was. I felt my worth. It was true that I lacked an Ivy League education. I came from small-town, backwoods USA. But while my father didn't make it past the second grade and my mother left school in the eighth grade, they weren't illiterate, silly, or stupid. They simply didn't have the opportunities—the exposure—that my classmates and colleagues and their parents had. Instead, they possessed wisdom from the School of Hard Knocks, wisdom from which I profusely benefited. I realized that even as I was evolving into a worldlier woman, I could continue to hold on to my roots.

The years of ambiguity shaped my reawakening and helped me redefine my identity without taking on a whole new one. When I looked around the Foreign Service, I saw a lot of capable, smart people, but very little representation of how America really looked back on the home soil. In the early 1990s, there were still few US diplomats of color. Women were a minority as well. I realized that in addition to my career path, it was important that I carve out a path wide enough for others to trail.

I threw myself into my responsibilities, staying past normal working hours to remain caught up, learning the jobs of people around me, and always being willing to help. Some of my bosses noticed; some didn't. The Foreign Service promotion system, for the most part, is a fair system. What I believe is that when I was promoted, it was because fair and honest supervisors who evaluated me did so based on my performance and potential, as well as my passion for what I did. My zeal is part of who I am, but it's also the reason *I am* who I am.

I didn't fare as well with those who struggled with a woman in an authority role or who couldn't see beyond the color of my beautiful pecan-tan skin. Some even had issues with my age.

I hate to say it, but people's personal preferences do get in the way of making decisions about others who are different than them. It happens, even in the Foreign Service, especially when I started over 27 years ago. I felt it and saw it, but I kept my mouth shut back then. An African-American colleague once said to me during a discussion about discrimination in the Foreign Service, "Vella, it's their sandbox; they allow us to come in to play. Because of it, they feel they can beat us down into the sand." I thought, *That's pretty freaking messed up*! Fortunately, as I became stronger in the system and understood the rules, I got up from the sand and pushed back.

Naturally, we all have preferences, including myself. I had to make some mental adjustments and meet people where they were—not where I thought they should be. It was crucial that I recognize my own preferences and work through them, and I believe wholeheartedly that most of my colleagues tried to do the same, but it is difficult to let go of what our parents and grandparents instilled in us.

I cannot say with certainty that each time I was passed over or denied something, it was due to prejudice against who I was. Nevertheless, I was denied or passed over, and it looked and smelled funky, but most of all, it hurt. When I saw my non-African-American and male colleagues getting promoted or getting what they asked for, when some were not nearly as qualified as I was, what was I to think? I did not want to become bitter or angry as I saw happen to some minorities. So, each time I felt slighted and wanted to say it was because of prejudice, I prayed and asked God to help me get over it quickly and find a way to position myself to not be passed over or denied the next time around. That was me, Vella from Holmestown, dealing with it. That said, I do not recommend others entering or who have been in the Foreign Service for a while to deal with it as I did most of my career. Use the resources available to try to deter or stop it.

I loved being overseas in plush places, for sure, but I was not truly convinced that I liked being in places that looked and felt like the United States. Communications worked reasonably well in First World countries, but that meant fewer opportunities to display my skills and abilities. So, I did one tour in Europe and decided that would be my last tour on a plush assignment. I went to Third World countries where there was always something to implement or tweak and there were high-level visits for a summit or conference I had to work. Working and living in those countries, I did not have the amenities of a First World country, but it was my strategy to excel. I worked it, and even though I did not escape what seemed and smelled like unfair treatment in some of those embassies, at least I was working my plan to succeed and had God as my partner, helping me deal with what came across my path in the interim.

That didn't mean I had to overlook mistreatment. From the start, I stood out—not for simply being black or a woman, but for my Southern accent. I didn't come across many deep Southerners serving in the State Department, and a Southern accent was considered "redneck" or "backwards" and, therefore, frowned upon. In fact, the few Southerners I knew had two accents: a work accent and the one they used when they returned home to the South. Tired of snide comments and eye-rolling, I did the same during those years I had lost sight of who I was. As I grew older and bolder, I paid no attention and was proud of my Southern accent. I became a part of letting the world know that the United States was a melting pot of accents, and the Southern American accent I possessed was one of them.

With some tours under my belt, I was assigned to Germany, a country where I encountered racism too bold to comprehend inside and outside the embassy. The great exodus of former communists from Russia and the displaced refugees from Turkey, Iran, and Iraq flooded to Europe, and into Germany, in particular, where people were frustrated and angry. Consequently, these minorities were treated as second-class citizens there. The same went for the few blacks I saw—there weren't many at the places I visited when I was assigned to Germany. The country was cold, and the Germans were rigid, in my opinion. Everywhere I looked, on the streets, in restaurants, at shopping malls, I saw no warm and inviting smiles. If my son reached to pet someone's dog, they slapped his hand away and spat nasty things toward him. Even though I did not speak much of the language, I could tell by the scorn on their faces that they thought my black son would contaminate their precious little dogs. For the first time, I had a good idea of what it must have been like to live in the South in the early 1900s.

The country's undercurrent of what I felt as racism etched its way into my relationships within the embassy. My immediate supervisor knew my strengths; his supervisor had been my supervisor in the Philippines. It was he who encouraged me to apply for a position in that country; my talents would be appreciated there, he said.

They were anything but. Despite having glowing recommendations and knowing that I was more than capable, I was given brainless, menial duties while a few select colleagues, one of whom was a white-male new hire, were given career-enhancing, substantive, and interesting duties. Everyone witnessed it and felt bad for me because they saw my eagerness to contribute more. I spoke up, but it did not help.

Finally, enough was enough. I bid on another position that would result in my assignment in Germany being cut short. The alternative was to quit, and I was not letting this good life for me and my son slip away. I prayed, and God paved the way for me to be selected to serve in another country. I had to leave Germany within weeks to begin the new assignment in Guatemala. My supervisor, who was out of the country when I applied for the new position, went ballistic when he returned and discovered I had requested to be transferred and that it was approved. He used profanity and called me names, some of which were derogatory terms for my race and gender. To this day, I cannot comprehend why he behaved this way since curtailment is common for many reasons in the Foreign Service. What I did understand was there were elements of bigotry in it all because he mentioned my race and gender when there was no need to.

Like many down South have done for so many years, I kept my mouth shut when I knew it would be slapped. I watched. I listened. I endured. But unlike many of them, I no longer felt less than my colleagues or that I should be degraded for something I honestly earned. Unlike before, I embraced who I was instead of trying to change or hide it. I had discovered that I was just as good as the next person, just as deserving, and I vowed to no longer sit quietly. No way was I going to quit like some of the colleagues who couldn't bear any more injustice. Instead, since I had reclaimed my voice and footing in Peru, I sought out ways to fight within the system if what I did and said was challenged and saw no rhyme or reason for it except bigotry.

One of the most effective ways to empower myself to fight back was to find mentors and really listen to what they were saying. One was my good friend from my assignment in Manila, a white male. I knew very few black communications colleagues back then, so I worked with the people who were there. I looked at the hearts and not the skin of those around me to find folks who would have my well-being and career at heart and did not feel challenged by me. He was one of those people, and I loved him dearly. He was married to a minority, so maybe that is why he felt compelled to help me. Who knows? He was a good man, and I allowed him into my world to help me, and he did. He used parables to teach me how to cope and get through situations without evading them. This relationship proved critical in the formative years of my career, when I later had two white men working for me who challenged my authority every chance they got. They made it obvious that working for a black woman wasn't something they wanted to do. I couldn't understand what made them feel and treat me this way. I was fair and nice to them, and we got along well when socializing, but in the office, it was a different story. They often worked only when they wanted to, and they said what they wanted to me at times. Of course, I would lash back, but not that hard and not all the time. I was strategic in that even though I had found my voice, I had to use it wisely.

When I explained my office dynamics to my mentor, he wrote back to me: "You have not done anything to elicit the behavior from them, Vella. Keep doing what you are doing. Remember, you are a black, young, Southern, beautiful, smart female—oh, and you are their boss. Think about that for second, Vella." That is all he wrote, and that was enough to make it crystal clear.

When I joined, there were fewer females in the Foreign Service than males, from my observation. There were even fewer in the IT and communications fields, and still even fewer of those were black. (Truth be known, there weren't many black *men*, either.) I recall how I met an African-American office manager in the Foreign Service who became a trusted friend. When back at the training center in the States after several overseas assignments, I had seen her around but declined having lunch with her several times, until one day she abruptly grabbed me by the arms and stopped me in the hall. It startled me.

"Girl, there are only a few of us," she said. "We need to stick together for support, and I need to school you on how to do it, because from what I see, you are doing this thing all wrong and will be disappointed down the road."

I was shocked by her forwardness. But it soon became apparent how right she was. She made me aware that the Foreign Service community was small, and the Foreign Service community of color was even smaller.

Another office manager became my second ally in the Foreign Service and a great friend, too. While working in the control room in Kampala for President Clinton's trip to Uganda in March 1998, I was admiring how well-dressed, regal, and confident this black female with a Southern accent was. Come to find out, she was admiring how I handled myself and how smart I was coordinating, fixing, and assisting some of the highest levels of the POTUS entourage—including President Clinton, when he graced us with his presence one evening in the control room where we worked.

This wonderful lady and I spoke during those few days in Kampala and had a nice meal together on the last day of the visit. "You are a together sister, Vella. You were working it this week," she said. Her praise made me feel so good, but then there was the "but." She said, "But girl, you have a little more work to do in order to prepare yourself for the blessings up ahead for you in this white organization." She went on to tell me things like how to dress smarter, how to not let folks take my glory, and how to use words that were more professional. Some may have been insulted, but I listened with the intent to apply what she said because deep within I knew that I had some unrefined edges. She was not just preparing me to be a professional black woman, but to stand out as a professional woman of color.

We became fast friends, and, through the years, she schooled me on how to dress better, hold my head higher, sit and walk more confidently, give trifling people certain looks and no words that confused them, put people in their place diplomatically, get to know the right people, and most of all keep my sanity to enjoy the amenities of the Foreign Service life when I was challenged.

What friends!

With those two women on each side of me, I could go nowhere but up. I called them my guardian angels. I learned to conduct myself with dignity, have pride in being an African-American female diplomat, and maintain a positive attitude amid the craziness that sometimes took place in the Foreign Service. Most of all, I learned how to reach up, down, laterally, or in any direction to encourage and help other females of color.

Neither woman was in the communications field as I was, but some years later, on a professional level, I got to know some of the few black females in my field. I admired one so much that she became a role model for me and did not even know it. *I want to be just like her,* I told myself after several encounters with her. I held on to that throughout my career. I saw how she handled herself in the communications field and was in awe. I looked for any opportunity to interact with her, hoping she would take me by the hands, as the other two sisters did, and tell me how to succeed in our field. She wasn't as forthcoming as I wanted her to be; however, that was fine because I listened, watched, learned, and emulated her every chance I got. I was going to be just like her, even if she did not give me one sentence of advice! Once, she chaired a briefing when I was on consultations in Washington. If someone had seen my face when she spoke there, they would have thought I was listening for how to discover precious jewels to get rich. She directed the meeting with confidence and command. She didn't have to speak loud or raise an eyebrow; she had the audience's respect. Even though she intimidated me, I wanted to be just like her. She inspired me.

No wonder, then, that I was overwhelmed when someone compared me to her. "You're going to be the next ... if you keep doing what you are doing, girl," a male colleague told me when talking about her in an admiring way after attending yet another meeting she chaired. I laughed, embarrassed, but I could see it.

Imagine how elated I was when she showed up at one of my assignments as a reemployed annuitant, my backup in a short-staffed office in a dangerous country. *OMG*, I thought, *she will see me in action as a boss woman. Will she be impressed with how I run my shop? Will she just sit back and do what she came to do? Will she give me advice?* I was a total wreck up to the day she arrived. We stepped out of the building to wait until the helicopter that transported her to the embassy landed. I stared at the door of the helicopter, heart racing fast and perspiring heavily in the heat from the helicopter and the environment. The door flung open, and there she was: my hero, here, to work side by side with me. I was humbled, but I felt my stars were lining up because there was no way she was going to be there for a month and I wouldn't learn something from her to help me be more successful in my career.

While my hero was still at post, Secretary of State Madeleine Albright visited that country. It was exciting times, and I wanted to be a part of it; I should have been a part of it as the communications officer. Unfortunately, my supervisor did not include me on the list of people to assist her visit at the airport—she was not coming to the embassy, but was going from her plane to a meeting not far from the airport with country officials. I was disappointed I had not made the list—communications is vital during these visits, so what the heck was my boss thinking when he excluded me? Yet just a few hours before her arrival, a small but significant communications snafu occurred. My supervisor pounded on the door, leaning on me to make it right. Time was of the essence.

With my hero's help, we resolved the issue, and my boss was relieved. At that moment, my hero nodded at me and looked at my supervisor. Without her speaking a word, I knew what I had to say and do.

"Sir, this was a close call, and if it had happened at the airport and you did not have your communications person there, it would reflect poorly on me, you, the ambassador, and the United States. I am getting my gear and going to the airport." I looked over at my hero because I was afraid to look at my supervisor in case he asked me if I was out of my freaking mind for speaking to him like that.

To my surprise, he said, "OK, I will see you there. Good job, Vella."

Thanks to the many conversations my hero and I had on how to properly show my talents and worth, and how to be an opportunist, I was ready to apply what she had taught me while she was there, right in front of her. Yes, I was going to be the next her.

Just as effective a tactic but one that I'm not as proud to share was learning to go with the flow—especially when going with the flow is not where I wanted to go. Many of my colleagues came from wealthy families. When they confronted an issue at work, oftentimes they'd simply turn matters over to their family lawyer. For people like me, with no legal recourse except the same system that screwed us over, we simply tried to make the system work for us or sucked it up. We kept quiet until we reached a level where we had authority to speak out and hope for changes. And then we had to be strategic in when and how we spoke out. That is why I said earlier that I now had my voice, but had to use it wisely. I did not want to get into a jam without expert help to get me out of it. I firmly believed in a Southern saying that I heard a lot growing up: "Do not let your mouth write a check your behind can't cash."

Midway through my career, when I underwent the excruciating humiliation of being escorted out of the US Embassy in Yaoundé, Cameroon, due to the suspension of my security clearance, I discovered the American Foreign Service Association (AFSA). They guided me throughout the ordeal. AFSA saved my career—and probably my life. I'd always advise young officers to try and work through issues on their own, but if it can't be done, know the resources at their fingertips, such as AFSA, the Office of Civil Rights, the Office of the Ombudsman, Human Resources Grievance, the Office of Special Counsel, and a few more. If there is discrimination, unfairness, bias, wrongdoing, retaliation, harassment—inadvertent or not—they will find it and make it right. Well, at least they made it right for me.

In a twist of irony, just a month before I retired, I received the State Department's Equal Employment Opportunity (EEO) Award. I received $10,000 and a beautiful signed plaque by Secretary of State John Kerry for EEO-related work I performed as a volunteer while assigned to the embassy in Tunisia. Can you imagine that? After all the time I had spent early in my career trying to be someone else to fit in or holding my tongue due to fear of being laughed at or treated unfairly, I received that high recognition for helping others be themselves, educating staff and management on diversity in the workplace, and using and promoting programs that I should have felt comfortable using myself when I was a victim. I am glad I was recognized. It was the perfect timing, and the recognition was one of the many reasons that when I walked out the doors of the Department of State on November 30, 2015, I had a pep in my walk, a smile on my face, and joy in my heart, while softly saying "looks like I made it" to myself.

You know, I believe a great many of us join the Foreign Service full of good values instilled in us from childhood, but upon retirement, those values are sometimes different, and we are someone else inside. We can no longer relate to family and friends, and, in some cases, it is tough even visiting or settling back into the community where we were raised. Of course, folks will change. For God's sake, I changed some. It is a part of life. But I never lost my identity, my compass—at least not for long. It was something precious to me. When I was recruiting for IT talent for the Foreign Service, I never hesitated to share my experiences with the young people I encountered. Indeed, it is one of the main reasons I wrote this book. I ask them, "Why? Why do you want to do this?" Answer that question with personal conviction and not to impress me, I tell them. It will serve as a compass when obstacles appear in your path. And they *will* appear.

I truly believe some officers, even though they're filled with enthusiasm about being a part of the Foreign Service, are afraid deep within. Accomplished as some may be, they worry about being Hispanic, Muslim, a woman, disabled, LGBTQ—they worry about being different. Just look at me, I tell them. I'm a black, Southern woman—that's three strikes, some would say—and yet it was only when I embraced my differences and especially my inner core—who I was—that I found a peace within myself. Feeling peace about my identity gave me confidence and allowed me to excel in the Foreign Service up until the day I retired. I am more than a number or a "token," as one of my colleagues who attended the Foreign Service new hire class referred to me on numerous occasions. "You were hired to meet a quota," he said. "Don't think you are all that, my dear." I would silently rebut him by thinking, *Yes, they needed a smart black woman, and I fit the bill.* I want those in the Foreign Service who are sometimes made to feel different to know they, too, are there to do more than just fill a quota. They are part of an organization whose strength is diversity, so their difference makes a difference.

I recall a few years back, when I was working in Washington, DC, a white male friend who was retiring stopped by my office to tell me good luck and goodbye. I asked him how he would cope in the real world after being a diplomat and living abroad for over 30 years. He came close to me and said in a low voice, "Vella, my friend, I joined, I worked, I enjoyed, but I never *became.*" He hugged me, shook my hands, turned his back, and walked out. That was profound to me. I was within retiring range, and I can't lie—thinking about how I would cope without the identity of being a US diplomat scared the heck out of me. I am so glad my friend stopped by to say goodbye because what he said jump-started the emotional part of my transition from the Foreign Service.

I interpreted his words to mean that he never lost sight of who he was. I truly needed to hear that because I was at a crossroads in my career. Did I want to wait around to hopefully be promoted to the ranks of the Senior Foreign Service (SFS), where

I would become more of a politician—which was not what I was or wanted to become? Or, over the next few years, did I want to set my target on retirement at age 55 and enjoy working toward obtaining just one more promotion that would place me at the highest grade level (grade 01) in the Foreign Service? Both were equally doable with a little time and hard work.

With the prestigious career I had, the decision should have been a no-brainer—fly and fly high until I could not fly any longer. Who in their natural mind would freely give up such a wonderful lifestyle and career when it was laid out before them for the taking for another 10 years? With me being "on fire" in my career, as several of my junior colleagues used to say, the sky was the limit. However, after that brief conversation with my friend and hearing the last phrase of his sentence—*but I never became*—play over and over in my head over the next few days, I knew which path to take.

It has always been a challenge for me to work in gray areas, even though I had to on many occasions in the Foreign Service. The Vella within, however, felt more comfortable with black and white. The SFS would be entering that gray zone. So, I decided to direct my energy toward completing my legacy as an accomplished Information Technical Manager without *becoming* a part of the gray zone. After I decided in my heart that was my path, I felt lighter and even bolder and more confident than ever. Those next three and a half years, I explored new things, like becoming a management officer, volunteering for an assignment in a war zone (Afghanistan), and turning my operations in the embassy over to junior staff while serving as a consultant to them—something that always stressed me, because while I wanted them to prepare for the next grade level, I needed my operation to run the way I wanted it to run since my name would be on the line.

Yep, a new Vella emerged—and I liked her! When the day came, I retired knowing in my heart that I did not *become* the Foreign Service. I only *worked* in the Foreign Service, thus my transition was joyful, smooth, and a blessing.

Vella, whose heart never truly left the muddy roads of Holmestown as she soared the blue skies of the world, now has her beautiful brown and gold Department of State retirement badge. I feel just as proud presenting my hard-earned retirement badge as I did presenting my diplomatic passport over 28 years ago, when I first joined the Foreign Service and folks looked at me with doubt that I was a US diplomat.

As proud as I was about my diplomatic passport and now about my retirement badge, I am most proud that I kept my identity— the most important of my values that helped me navigate through the Foreign Service to retirement.

Lastly, I say to those who enjoy the Foreign Service (or whatever organization they work for), but sometimes feel like quitting or crawling under a rock when others, inadvertently or not, make them feel as if their identity/difference is a bad thing or they do not belong: Do not hesitate to tell them it hurts, and they need to stop. If it continues, use the available resources set up for making it stop. Embrace your identity. Never quit a job you enjoy because you are afraid to speak out against those who treat you unfairly because of your difference. Know where you want to go, and don't worry about whether you fit the mold. And above all, remember and embrace who you truly are, making where you come from—physically or within your heart—work for you, not against you.

CHAPTER 7

Friends and Family

Those who keep your secrets, call them a friend.
Those who accept your flaws, call them family.
Everyone else, call them a work in progress.

I love my family, and I love a family environment. This inten-sified when I was serving my country abroad. Not because I missed home, but because family will love and support you no matter what; at least mine did most of the time. Therefore, it was no surprise that I instilled a sense of family in my team at every embassy I worked in.

One of the most shocking revelations I had in the Foreign Service was realizing how many people aren't in touch with their families back home. When I joined, there was no such thing as internet and social media, so staying connected required patience and a small fortune in long-distance phone charges. But today, with Skype, WhatsApp, and FaceTime, staying in touch with family while abroad has gotten much easier.

Coming from an outspoken, large and close-knit family like mine, I never realized that I had a choice to see my family or not.

Growing up, Mom rarely let us out of the yard to play with other kids. She was so afraid of us going astray, as some kids in the community had, that she kept us at home—on serious lockdown.

"Your sisters and brothers are your friends! Don't bother me with this friend or stupid baseball game mess. There's enough of y'all nappy heads here to play with each other, and the yard is plenty big enough to play any kind of game there is with each other." That was her response when we would tell her that we wanted to have friends over or go walking down the muddy dirt road with cousins and friends to the baseball park.

In her mind, we'd best figure out how to get along because no one knows us like our brothers and sisters, and we would be stuck with them for life, or at least until we found a way to leave home. And she was right. Luckily, for those of us who were still at home during the prison-like lockdown period, we were only one to three years apart in age, so we had things in common. But most of all, because Momma kept us close to each other, we bonded as friends as well as siblings, for life.

Momma was hard on us, in part because that's the only way she knew how to parent. Her mother died when she was barely 5 years old. She never remembered being held or cared for by her own mother, so I suppose it was hard for her to show us a level of maternal love that she had never experienced herself. Instead, her oldest sister, Lucille, served as a surrogate mother to help raise her, pushing and prodding her along as best she could. Naturally, that's mostly how Momma parented us.

During my stint back in my parents' home during my failing marriage to Tim, Momma never let up on me, reminding me loud and clear, with a little cussing in between, that I was wasting my life with him. She was disgusted with my wallowing and

116

disappointed with my choices. But she never closed the door. She'd say, "You might come home with your head down, but you come home before someone finds you and that child dead on the street somewhere. You ain't homeless, child!" Her favorite line when admonishing me was: "Child, I do not care what happened. All I know is you better get your tail back home before I come there and beat you all the way back to Holmestown." Ironically, this line truly made me never hesitate to come home. That was a rough-loving Momma talking—telling you that you screwed up but in the same breath telling you to come home, if needed.

I often try to emulate my mom in raising Andrew, especially about family and coming home. I hope he is hearing me because I know he loves his family, but, to date, it seems like he has not grown roots in family. Lord have mercy, it worries me when I think how isolated he is in the world. Recently, after our last annual family reunion (on my mother's side), he and I talked about family when we had time for each other. I told him that since he had such a good time the last few times he came home for the event, he should keep in touch more with folks. He looked at me as if I did not know what I was saying and said, "Momma, I do keep in touch with family—I call Grandma every chance I get, and I do not know if you know this or not, but the younger folks in the family communicate on a regular basis. You know Kayla, Virginia, Juan Jr., Sally, Maria, and I have always been close."

I hugged him and whispered while patting him on the back, "That is great, son, but just know when the going gets rough, you can always come home to Momma to regroup. I love you—family loves you no matter what."

That reassurance is all I had to hold on to in some of my loneliest and scariest moments overseas. In Bonn, Germany, where I felt the most detached from my colleagues, work, and family. I wanted to give up on the Foreign Service. *Enough of this already*, I would think as I forced myself out of my warm bed to face another cold day, imagining myself marching into the HR office and asking them to send me and my child home for good. Things in Germany were dreary and cold all the time—the weather, most of my fellow Americans in the embassy, and the local people. The two things that made me feel warm inside and out—and kept me going besides the great German beer and bratwurst sausages— were coming home at the end of the workday to a warm hug from my son and knowing that if I packed him up and returned home to Holmestown yet again, my mom would be fine with it. I would get a good cussing out, but afterward, things would be fine, and I would find another way out.

Daddy was also tough, but he let Momma administer the discipline most of the time. After she had worn us out verbally, physically, or both, he'd come in quietly and tell us that we needed to listen to her. He worked his entire life, dropping out of second grade to help his sharecropper parents on the farm. Later, he did stints as a longshoreman, lumberjack, and pulp mill worker, among other odd jobs. There wasn't much money. There wasn't much to look forward to except on Friday evenings when he got paid. Like clockwork, his friends would show up before or shortly after he came home, and they'd sit out under their favorite tree, drinking until the whiskey or weekend ran out. It drove my mother crazy because he'd often drink up his paycheck or take out a high-interest loan at the Hinesville Bank when he felt like having a chunk of money in his pocket to blow. This left Momma with barely enough to feed us and pay the bills in the week ahead. I remember the anger and worry in her eyes, pissed and afraid the electricity would get cut off or there would be no money to buy our staple foods—rice, sugar, grits, potatoes, beans, flour, onions, cooking oil—to feed us (meat was a luxury). Nevertheless, she could make a dollar stretch. I still recall the instant disappointment I felt when she would tell me she wasn't sure if she and Daddy could afford to buy exactly what I needed for school or anything at all. Then, before I knew it, magic happened. She found the money.

Somehow, Momma made it work, but it was rough. That money Momma magically made appear did not literally drop out of heaven into her lap. I eventually found out that Momma was a wheeler and dealer in the background, selling brews and playing the numbers to make ends meet. Daddy was aware of this—hell, he bought her brew himself—and maybe that is why he did not have a second thought about wasting his hard-earned money whenever he wanted to live a little. He knew Momma would not let the family go completely hungry nor neglect to get his kids what they needed to succeed in life.

I never wanted to know that feeling of insecurity as an adult or let Andrew be the recipient of it. When I began making my own money, I vowed to always count on money I brought in and not depend on someone else's—not even a husband's—as my primary source of income to take care of me and my child and the bills. No way. I'd take care of it all myself.

By the time I got to college, Momma had a little stash of money in the black folks' credit union down in Midway, Georgia. What Daddy, my older siblings, Mr. Herman or Mr. Albert could not contribute to financing my education, Momma rose to the occasion and dug into her credit union money to help. In hindsight, I should have understood more when she got blood mad with me after I landed a good-paying job and a husband, and then told her that Tim asked me to reduce the monthly stipends I sent to her so we could afford to send the same to his mother, too. Oh my God, I remember when I told her. I was sitting on the couch of my apartment in Seaside, California, on a beautiful day, staring into the ether and thinking *This is so nice—I am a college graduate with a husband, a good job, and enough money to financially support family back home in Georgia.* So, I expected Momma to embrace what I told her—her baby girl was a provider. However, when I got the words out, there was a silence as long as eternity followed by Momma saying, "What the hell are you talking about, girl?" That jolted me so hard, I feel the shock in my bones whenever I think of it—even right now, I had to stop a second to regroup. I learned that if we crossed the line with money Momma said was due to her, all hell broke loose. Daddy, on the other hand, accepted whatever we put in his hands. He was easygoing and appreciative.

After all was said and done, I became a responsible adult and embraced those valuable lessons learned from both parents. I am still applying them as well as passing them on to Andrew and even my grandchildren, little Keegan, Ian, and Anah. My parents did what they thought they needed to do within their respective roles, and I love them equally. They were simple and ordinary people playing an extraordinary role in the making of Vella, the diplomat. They were very wise to rear us to be responsible, hard-working, respectful, respected, and God-fearing.

Yes, they were both wise. What I saw and heard from them while growing up shaped my character and my future as a US diplomat. When Momma sensed I did not want to walk the muddy road to complete a chore or go to church, she would say, "Girl, you better

120

start walking down that road. You'll forget it's muddy and feel it is a part of you when you get to moving on it." "Walk it now and you'll be able to get a car later to ride in," I heard her say a few times. It made no sense to me back then, but she was so right. Those muddy roads made me who I am today. I am proud to have had my humble beginnings on those roads in Holmestown. I proudly walked them back then because I knew that there was a great big ol' world waiting for me to discover for the rest of my life, far beyond those dirty muddy roads. So, I heeded and listened and learned from any and everything my parents said.

My relationships with my brothers and sisters are also something to boast about, even though some are more complicated than others. My brothers, all six of them, love to show off their baby sister. When I was a teenager, they made me feel special by saying I was smart and I was going to do big things in life.

Douglas, my eldest brother (deceased), reared by my Aunt Lucille and Uncle Peter in Florida, gave me my first opportunity to see the world outside of Georgia. During several summers when I was in high school, he would come to get me in Georgia and take me back with him to MacDill Air Force Base in Tampa, Florida, where he was stationed. Some of the family members were afraid of him because he was strict and was quick to strike them. I loved being with Douglas because he treated me like a princess. He was bold and courageous, just like Momma. "Picky head, you're my favorite sister. I love you, and you make something of yourself, you hear me girl?" he'd say.

Douglas always told me to watch out for boys and to not let

them sweet talk me and get me pregnant. He would say, "Get an education and a career first, and the good stuff in life will come. Men and kids are the good stuff, but if you get either of them before you make something of yourself, you will ruin your life." I wasn't sure what he was talking about most of the time back then, but whatever came out of my beloved big brother's mouth mattered to me, and looking back, I so appreciate his concerns and care. Now that I am a grown black woman with valuable life experience, I fully understand the message and some of the values he was instilling in me—intelligence, confidence, patience, and a sense of family. If he were still alive, I know he would be proud of his baby sister.

Steven, my second-eldest brother, was regimented, just like his big brother Douglas, and still is. He was a second father to us since Douglas was raised in another household far away from us. I do not recall during my childhood ever knowing Steven to joke around. When he spoke, I listened in fear. Others feared Douglas, but I feared Steven. Due to the father-like image he portrayed, when I was in trouble as a child and young adult and was afraid to go to Daddy or Momma, I went to him. If it weren't for Steven (and his loving wife, Sharon), I would have missed the opportunity to serve in the Foreign Service. When I was invited for the Foreign Service Oral Assessment, I was literally penniless. I called Steven, who at the time was stationed in Fort Lee, Virginia, and asked if he could lend me money for gas and food. This was after I explained my pipe dream of working in Washington, DC, to him. He never told me I was crazy, it was a long shot, or anything negative. What he said was: "Baby sis, you are smart enough. If that's your dream and you think you can do this, let me speak with Sharon and get back with you,

OK?" What I loved and still love about Steven is that he respects his wife as an equal partner and never makes a financial move without consulting her. He talks trash to her, but when it comes to business, they are a team.

That night, Steven called me back and told me that $300 for gas and food was waiting for me at Western Union, and they sent a few dollars extra. I said, "Thank you, thank you, thank you, Steven. Tell Sharon thank you, too. I will pay you guys back and will never forget it." When I hung up the phone, I was so dang scared because I did not know what I would face at the Oral Assessment. I immediately wanted to call Steven back and say never mind, I am not going and am returning your money. However, instantly I heard these words Steven said to me during the initial phone call I made to him: *Baby sis, you are smart enough, so if that's your dream and you think you can do this ...* Steven, you know what, big bro? That was my dream, and I got that job, thanks to not only the money you and Sharon made available to me to make the trip, but also those words you spoke to me. Those words placed life into my dream of traveling and placed courage in my heart to face the unknown out there. Because of that fear I instantly had after you told me the money was sent and the fear of letting you down after what you just did for me, I made the trip to Washington and eventually the journey through the Foreign Service. What I am saying is: your hard-earned dollars took me to Washington, DC, my smarts got me the job, and having continued encouragement and support from family like you sent me into the world fearlessly to conquer it.

Lots of family members supported me while on my journey, but Steven and Sharon planted the initial seed. When Steven retired from the military and his finances decreased, I voluntarily started sending him a monthly stipend to supplement his retirement check until he found work. He was adamant about me not giving him my hard-earned money, but it was a losing battle for him. I was determined to share my earnings because his hard-earned salary made a way for me to get mine. I was proud and told him not to deny me my blessing of blessing him. I wanted to show my appreciation even after so many years. I believe that is when he gave in and said, "OK, baby sis, since you put it like that, my wife and I will accept the blessing." I remember where we were standing when we had the conversation—it was in his backyard, where he was holding a wrench, pausing from performing mechanical work on his car, and Sharon had a rake in her hands, pausing from raking her yard. They both came and hugged me. I left quickly so they could not see the tears of joy stream down my eyes for that blessing. What a team, and what a big brother!

And then there are the twins, Ryan and Ronald, polar opposites. Ryan got me out of Holmestown to start a new life when he asked me to come to California to live with him and his family after I graduated from college. He did not have to ask me twice. My suitcase was packed months before graduation, and I saved all my pennies to buy a one-way ticket.

On the West Coast, Ryan loved introducing me as his "smart baby sister." When we were serving abroad in the same country—he in the United Nations (UN) and I in the Foreign Service—the introduction changed to his "smart diplomat sister." Unfortunately, he has capitalized on his bragging over the years by soliciting my help with the complicated financial issues of working for an international organization like the UN. So many times, I have wanted to say, "Please do not bother me; figure it out yourself, get a lawyer, ask someone else in the family. I am busy," but my heart leads me to do it for him—time and again. I think it is not just because he is my brother who opened his doors and pockets to me to start my life after college away from Holmestown, but because he has an easy and giving heart, just like me. When I see him, I see me! So, guess what, Ryan? I got your back!

Ronald, my dear brother Ronald. He is the self-proclaimed "clever one" of the twins. I have always admired him for doing what he wanted to do in life. As far back as I can remember, I have had a good relationship with him. I know he loves me like there is no tomorrow, and I love him right back, but I'm also smart enough to know that he'd talk his way into my pocketbook for his personal gain without giving it a second thought if I wasn't on my p's and q's around him.

Ronald has spent several stints behind bars. My nephew Frank and I went to his out-of-town court appearance when he first met up with trouble, and I visited him when he was locked up. Silly me and my love for him: I even wrote to the warden the last time he was incarcerated to plead for his release—me, his little sister. Whenever I would do a kind act for him, he'd smile and say, "Thank you, Jane. You will get this blessing back one day in abundance." Guess what, big brother? God did bless me—with you and the rest of my other siblings who I know will have my back, if needed. Keep doing you!

Harold, a few years younger than the twins, was raised by Aunt Lucille and Uncle Peter along with Douglas in Florida. They didn't visit us in Georgia very often, so I didn't get a chance to know him well until I was in the Foreign Service and had the resources to go and visit him in Florida. I would hug him tight and put a few dollars in his hands before I would zip off to my next country of assignment in the Foreign Service. I know he did not need the money I placed in his hands since he had a good job, but my heart led me to share with him. In hindsight, I hope I did not embarrass him. Big bro, I gave out of love!

He, too, said, "Thank you, baby sis! God will continue to bless you for being so kind and giving. Be safe with all that traveling. Don't know how you do it, but if you are happy, keep doing it, sis."

My brothers are faithful Christians, and I held their words close to my heart as blessings. During my rough times, instead of feeling hopeless, I should have remembered that those blessings they wished upon me were coming.

And boy, did they come. I survived two bad marriages, weathered a complicated high-pressure position in the Foreign Service, resiliently endured the threat of being fired from the civil service and downgraded in the Foreign Service, and, with barely a scratch, escaped several terrorist attacks abroad and domestically on facilities I was in. Also, awards and recognitions, promotions, a blessed son, houses, great lifelong friends, cars, a great husband (eventually), awesome grandchildren, and now retirement are among other blind blessings they spoke of that materialized and streamed my way.

What I now know with certainty, because I am a living testimony to it, is that if anyone says, "God bless you" to me, that blessing will surely come. So, I tell anyone who hears those words spoken to them to please graciously thank the person saying them because the blessing(s) will come when least expected.

Speaking of blessings, I am glad to be blessed with Eugene Jr., or just "Junior," my baby brother. Junior is slow-moving and cautious. He rarely takes sides and tries to see the good in everyone. If he does take a side, it is after he has thoroughly analyzed the entire situation.

Momma relies on Junior heavily in her old age. He still spends a great deal of his time with her, taking her to the bank and grocery shopping and doing odd jobs around the house. He also listens to her fussing and complaining about other members of the family and even complaining about him to his face. Recently, when I was home and Momma was giving him a hard time, as if he were a child, I asked him: "Junior, how can you stand it, baby brother?" He told me that many years ago, he made a promise to God that he would take care of Momma under any circumstances until one of them leaves this earth. He is doing it. I am grateful, and I am sure Momma is, too.

Junior spent the first part of his career in the military, going in as a strapping good-looking teenager ready to take on the world and coming out wiser and prayerful. Baby brother always maintains a great spirit, even when my siblings rib him for staying under Momma's coattails and putting up with her when she is being critical. I've always been thankful that he has lingered around, because with Momma in her elderly years, it gives me comfort to know that Junior will be there when she calls. And she's not the easiest person to live with. Even so, he plods along happily, unfazed by her constant complaints and nagging. Just this summer, when Momma chided him about wanting to get married—at age 53—he assured her that he would not leave or forget about her even if he did marry his girl.

Now, those sisters of mine are a handful. Because I was the youngest girl, my sisters felt they could push me around. On the other hand, because I was the youngest girl, I was mothered and protected by them.

Loren Ann, the oldest sister by 17 years, applauded my

achievements and was appreciative of whatever I did for her. She passed away in 2001, but I have lots of good memories of my big sister.

It is no secret that Loren grew up wearing hand-me-downs or handmade clothes most of the time, I suppose since money wasn't plentiful back then. She loved when I brought her jewelry and clothes from my travels around the world. A pretty woman who flaunted her femininity, she would tear open the gift wrap and then prance around clutching the pair of earrings, necklace, or scarf to her chest before she put it on. She was the first of my sisters who truly embraced the gifts I brought them from my travels.

Because of her birth order as the oldest, Loren protected us. Once, when a girl teased me on the school bus for wearing hand-me-downs, Loren was at the bus stop the next day. I knew what was about to go down and smiled at the bully of a girl as I rushed off the bus.

"Did that little 'B' tease you again?" she asked.

"Yeah," I admitted.

When the bus driver drove off, Loren grabbed my hand and marched me down the road to the kid's house and dared her or any other family member to come outside.

No one came out. So, as we walked back home, Loren told me not to let anyone walk over me.

"Look cute, but be tough and kick some butt when you have to, baby sister," she'd say. She taught me what to tell people or how to act tough if they bothered me. She used to say, "And if that don't work, kick 'em in the stomach, hard, and don't run." I do not think she was violent by nature; she was just teaching me some survival techniques. Yep, that was my big sister.

Even in adulthood, she continued to look after me in other ways by telling me how to distinguish the good and bad types of friends or what types of men to stay away from. I hold those sister-to-sister brief and awkward teaching conversations with her dear to my heart to this day. Big sis, if you can hear me: ain't no one walking over me, thanks to you.

Rachel and I are 16 years apart. She is a hybrid between a mother and sister to me. An icon in the Holmestown community due to her nurturing and kind nature, she has lived in the same house her husband, "Bubba" bought them a few years after they got married. He was one of my daddy's drinking partners. I love that old man. He was very funny and used to make me laugh all the time. He used to slip some dollars to me when I was in college. "Use this to buy you a notebook and pencils in school," he would say.

During heated arguments between my daddy and momma, when I was in my early teen years, I'd get frustrated and scared, so I'd jump out of my bedroom window and run to Rachel and Bubba's house down the street. She'd drive or walk me back home and smooth things over. At every stage of my life up to present and regardless of what I was experiencing, Rachel's love and support made me feel that I was not alone in it.

Rachel appreciates everything I do for her and never asks me for anything. She accepts tokens of money after I insist. Accepting gifts from around the world, especially dresses from Africa, is another story. She dares me not to come home without them or else. She loves them, but it took her a while to warm up to them—unlike Loren who loved whatever I brought her from the beginning.

Despite the poor conditions we grew up in, Rachel has managed the impossible, to make her home a haven where everyone feels comfortable and loved. Somewhat like Momma, Rachel took in destitute relatives, fed them if they were hungry, or did kind acts for them to make them feel whole again. These days, Momma and Rachel often go at each other, but it is not because they do not love and respect each other—it is because they are so much alike. They even look alike.

On long nights overseas, I'd wish for 10 minutes to sit on Rachel's couch. I dreamed of being there, eating a big plate of collard greens, rice, and neck bones while telling her and anyone else in the house my Foreign Service stories between bites.

"Slow down before you choke, Jane; the food is not going to run away," I imagined her saying. "I cooked it for you—there's plenty more in the pot." She tells me the same thing to this day: "I cooked enough food to go around, so do not rush. Slow down, chew your food properly, or else you will never lose weight, girl." Again, that's her, loving and caring.

Emma is a different type of big sister than Loren and Rachel. She could be considered the middle child—midway between the two big sisters and two younger sisters. To me, she has an unexplainable passion to be in control. She is a formidable and take-charge type of woman, but with a kind heart. Unfortunately, she had a lapse in kindness when, as I mentioned earlier, I was down on my luck and asked her to help me pay my light bill, and she refused.

In retrospect, I am glad Emma did not bail me out at that dark time in my life because it taught me a lesson. It taught me to think things through and be prepared to accept the consequences of bad decisions. I promised myself that I would never ask her for money again, and I do not recall ever asking her; however, that is not to say I never accepted monetary gifts she freely gave to me.

Through the years, Emma has challenged me to go higher and bigger—the next level, but at her fast and sometimes nerve-wracking pace, not mine. She moves a hundred miles an hour when she gets excited about a prospect for her or anyone else. My speed is more a cross between a turtle and a rabbit—calculated and paced initially, but quick and focused to the finish line.

When I would come home on vacations, I loved nothing more than letting my hair go wild and walking around on bare feet or in flip-flops. Emma could hardly stand it and often dragged me to the beauty salon or brought me a nice pair of sandals or shoes to wear because they were "cute." I knew her intent and enjoyed the pampering, but each time I came home, I wanted to slow it down and become Jane from Holmestown, not Vella the Diplomat.

As an accomplished business owner, pastor, and community leader, it's obvious she likes to be out front. I admire Emma when she goes out in the community and encourages others to excel and get involved—except when it involves me. It just so happened there would always be a meeting, a lunch, or another event for her to attend whenever I would be home on vacations. "Get dressed and come with me, Jane," she would say. "I will be there in an hour. Oh, and I bought a dress for you to wear. Size 10, right?"

There were doctors, lawyers, politicians, pastors, and other social-ites and community leaders for me to meet. She thought she was slick, but I didn't buy into her plans. I don't know if she knew that I was content to sit in the ditch or under the tree in Momma's yard and talk with the perceived ne'er-do-wells like Butch or Papa Joe. I honestly think she did not know how much it meant to me to hang out with these guys when I returned home. I loved being with them, because I knew they were proud that I made it out and made it big. I felt like I was their hero, and they treated me as such. When I would tell them I had to return overseas, they would say, "Go represent Holmestown, home girl." Sharing a beer and sausage with them in the ditch meant more to me than sipping wine while dining with the most prestigious person in Georgia.

Emma believes in action and moving—now. It's not enough to think about an opportunity—she insists that I need to pursue it now, now! There have been times that her directness has been extremely overwhelming. For instance, I told her that I was writing my memoir, and before I got my last thought out to her, she was envisioning me sharing my story with the world on *Oprah* and imagining Tyler Perry working with me to make a movie from the manuscript.

Emma has pushed me as far back as I can remember. She saw potential in me before I saw it in myself. She has made me pursue opportunities with conviction, and I owe part of my professional success and personal growth and development to her. I am so glad she now has her own grown black girls to push around. I need a break from that sister.

My sister Brittany—we call her Hattie—is a year older than me. As girls, we went at it a lot, but were inseparable—best friends. We went to Albany State College together. We went to the clubs and partied together. We worked at the same restaurant together as teenagers—our first jobs. She had asked her boss, Winston, to hire me, and he did. She loved me and has always looked out for me, even after she married Juan, a military guy. He took her away from me, but we kept in touch, and it was nothing to open a letter from her while I was still in college to find a money order or a little bit of cash in it. Some months ago, I ran across an old letter she had written to me while I was at Georgia Southern College, telling me that she heard about my good grades last semester.

It said that she had tucked in $50 and promised to send more when she got paid. What a sister. Even today, she takes care of me. If I drive up to her house with a dirty car, she cusses me out and rushes in the house to get her cleaning supplies to wash my car—with her own hands. Awesome sister who I truly appreciate.

When Andrew returned to the States to attend boarding school, Brittany became his surrogate mother, since she was closer to him geographically than my other siblings. I am so thankful to her for taking care of not just him, but Virginia too. (Virginia is Rachel's granddaughter and my godchild. I had legal guardianship over her at the time, and she was in boarding school with Andrew.) Some years later, I was able to return the favor by being there for Maria, her only daughter, when she needed to get out of a toxic situation when she was in college. We reciprocated our kindness to each other back in the day with no hidden agenda. We were sisters—we helped each other no matter what.

Brittany and I were the perfect sisters up until about the last 10 years. I thought we had simply grown apart since I had gotten so focused on my job and came home less often, our kids were grown, she was divorced, and I had remarried. However, a few years ago I started becoming the "other" sister and took verbal lashings from her for unexplainable reasons. I was baffled and started asking myself and my husband: "What did I do to her?" There were no answers, just an increase in what seemed like hatred toward me. She even told me once to never set foot on her property again simply because I told another sister to tell her congratulations for building and moving into her new home. As tolerable as I had become of family members, my heart could not take the pain from what she said. So, I honored her wish and stayed away, thinking she would reach out to me when she was ready for me to come back. We would do casual greetings and conversations at family gatherings she and I attended—which were not many. I called her for her birthdays and major holidays, but she never picked up the phone and never returned the calls. That hurt, but I kept doing it.

Then, in 2017, when planning for the family reunion, I received a phone call from her telling me that she received the family reunion letter and that she and her two kids and granddaughter Nancy were going to come. That conversation was the beginning of a comeback for our close relationship, but at a price. Since that call, I have repeatedly listened attentively for hours to her pouring her heart out to me about the reasons for her lashing out at me and her voluntary separation from other family members. She shared all of it—the good, the bad, and the ugly. Some of her reasons were shocking to me while others I suspected but wasn't sure about. Some of the things about me, she had every right to be upset about even though I did not intend them as malicious toward her, but some of the things were just life unfolding, and I didn't deserve the lashings of anger from her. Nevertheless, they were her feelings and emotions, so I listened. I am still listening. I guess it will take a while to hear it all, but I am retired and a good listener. So, I listen, still!

I want her to be made whole again with me, but even more, I want our kids and grandkids to get close like we were and will be again. I believe in miracles, and I do believe over the past year, thanks to the Way Family Reunion 2017 planning, we are on the path to a healthy and lasting relationship. We will always be sisters; it is the friendship I crave to be restored without caveats. I think it is what she wants too because at one point early in this healing process, she cussed me out the good old-fashioned way. The next day she called back and asked me to forgive her because she had a lot within her to get out about the topic we were on. That returned call and apology from her spoke volumes about who this sister, my sister Brittany, really is deep within. So, I listen, still.

I can't talk about family without including my soul sister, Heather. I can't recall when I met her for the first time, but what I do remember is that we have been friends for as long as I can remember. She is a year younger than me, and while she recently proclaimed for the first time that I'm bossy, I've never been able to boss her around. At least, I did not feel like I was bossing her around. Even so, she has remained my friend all these years, and a few years back we declared each other our best friend forever (BFF) *and* family. We ushered together in church, went to the same high school, danced like hell at the enlisted men's club (the Zoo) at Fort Stewart, graduated from the same college, and each had only one son who has given us wonderful grandchildren. After college, she married an awesome local guy and became a respected hometown banker and socialite in our county. After college, I chose to leave Georgia behind to pursue my dreams of traveling the world. To this day, she has never lived anywhere else since we met, and while I'm disappointed that she hasn't gotten to see the world along with me, she has given me something else to look forward to when I come home—visiting and hanging out with her. And though she has not traveled the world, she tells others that she has done so vicariously through my stories.

When I lived overseas, she would call me: "Long time girl, how are you? When are you coming home again?" Our conversations were short, but just enough to catch up on what mattered in our lives.

Closer to my visit, she'd call again and ask, "Hey girl, tell me again when you will be home?"

"For Easter," I would respond if that was the case.

"Oh, good. What type of food are you craving?" An excellent cook, she would have an elaborate menu planned as a treat for my homecoming. I absolutely loved it. I wasn't a big eater, but Heather could not tell it because I ate two servings of everything, as if I had not eaten in a few days. It was like eating at Rachel's house. I ate fast and plentiful.

I recall in 2016 when I was preparing to go back to DC after visiting Georgia for Thanksgiving, Heather called to tell me she was disappointed that I could not stop by her house to share a meal. She asked what time we were going to leave for DC. I told her it was going to be early in the morning and that the only stop we would be making before reaching South of the Border (in South Carolina) to rest and fill up was at the gas station down the street in Midway before getting on I-95 headed north. She went quiet and said, "Darn, shoot." Then she said that she would meet us there in the morning. Thinking she was crazy to get up that early, I had a lapse in memory as to what a true and good friend she was. She met us there the next morning and, oh my goodness, she came with two boxes of prepared food. One with pies and cupcakes, three types of slices of cakes, and some oranges. The other one, which I called the "BFF box," had foiled-over dishes of neck bones and pig tails, roasted beef, baked mac and cheese, rice, cabbage, cornbread, etc. She even had real cutlery, hot sauce, napkins, and plates. I stood there in the cold, tearing through foil, taking a bite of everything. When I got to the neck bones and pig tails, I poured hot sauce on them and started jumping and swaying from side to side, eating like a madwoman. She laughed and said, "You do not know how much joy it gives me to see you enjoy eating my food." I lifted my head, spit out a bone, and smiled while diving back in for more.

I would have eaten the entire bowl if Shaka had not blown the horn and screamed, "Stop eating, and let's go, Vella." I grabbed the boxes out of Heather's car and placed them in our vehicle. I ran back over to Heather's car and gave her a big hug and thank you. One thing is for sure: if I ever move back home, I will never go hungry if my BFF is around. Love her, and her food, too.

Overseas, I missed my soul sister just as much as my blood sisters. Nevertheless, there was a time when I was glad that we were separated because I did not know what to think of our relationship. I was deeply offended by something she had said when I needed a friend. Because of it, I spent years holding back the deep, dark parts of my life that I needed a soul sister's listening ear or counsel for. Then, a few years ago I opened up to her about it and declared to her that it was the reason I only shared the good things in my life with her. She told me that she did not recall the incident, and it was probably because she had her own issues around the same time. We worked through it and, henceforth, vowed to have open hearts and ears for each other, no matter what. To me, that was the defining moment in our relationship that moved her beyond my soul sister to my BFF, the keeper of my secrets.

———————

Leaving a big family behind made it hard to go overseas. I always felt that I was detached and on my own in the world, but the reality was just the opposite. Andrew and I had never been completely on our own while living overseas. We could always call Momma or a sibling to look through my mail for letters that needed a quick response, send a new pair of sneakers for Andrew, guide my first home purchase, let me use their mailing address to ship boxes, buy me boxes of my favorite detergent or sausages when they were on sale so I could take them back overseas the next time I was home, send me care packages of all sorts of goodies, and whatever else I could not do from the Philippines or the 12 other countries I served in overseas. Without them, I am not sure how I would have managed my home affairs.

Then, there was the need for peace of mind while abroad. If I couldn't have had my blood kin with me for relief, I'd have to create a family from friends, staff, and colleagues. For example, Andrew's nanny, Katie, came highly recommended to us in the Philippines, so I did everything I could to let her know how much I valued and appreciated her. I treated her like family and told her she was family, and she, in turn, became family to us. Andrew loved her so much that she joined us as his nanny during our stint in Bonn, Germany.

For each assignment after that, I made it my mission as a mother to find a nanny I not only trusted, but could accept as family. Upon arriving in a new country, I went to great lengths interviewing to find the perfect person. We had hardworking Katie in the Philippines and Germany, motherly Flora in Peru, caring but stern Gloria in Guatemala City, and stern Aunty Ethel in Tanzania, Uganda, and Cameroon. Andrew was never alone; the nannies loved him, and we loved them. Nevertheless, I was always peeping and listening to ensure he was OK, even though I knew I had chosen good nannies. It was the mother and the Foreign Service security training in me, I suppose. He was my joy—my baby boy, and I did not want to miscalculate a nanny and discover later that she neglected or abused him. I got lucky. They were all good people whom I trusted my son and house to while I made a living working eight to 12 hours a day, if not longer when the need arose.

While I would have liked to be more connected to the cities and communities where I lived abroad, I opted not to for personal and professional reasons. Often my workload did not allow for it. Few other professionals worked as many hours as we did in the IT field, so if I did have time in the evening, it was usually later, when "normal" people were home with their families. Truth be known, early on, the security briefings we received before moving to a new country scared me to death. I was guarded, and rightly so, but it made it hard to strike up a casual friendship with a local outside the embassy perimeter walls. That changed over time as I became a more experienced and vigilant diplomat and traveler.

This led to me building a network around me, which I called my "surrogate family," to help me get through the days and years abroad. I am not an open and inviting person by nature, so if someone was allowed in my personal sphere—and there were only a few—they were lucky and well-vetted.

Colleagues at the office wanted to get to know me better. Many wanted to get to know me outside of work, but they knew my primary commitments and priority time slots were for work and my son. Despite not permitting most of them in my personal sphere, I ensured they knew they could depend on me and that I was in the trenches with them—as a boss and colleague. I allowed them to be extended families, as needed. Sometimes, folks who were not in my personal sphere needed a listening ear, and I am not one to turn my back on folks when the walls are falling in on them, especially when they're away from their family and friends. I listened to them, cried with them, and then pointed them to resources I thought would be helpful. When the crisis was over, they were thankful but knew it did not mean we were friends.

Most of the locals appreciated my style and cautiously bought into the family idea. They knew Momma Vella was nice and friendly, but did not like slackers. So, they played hard with me and worked hard for me. Some even went the extra mile and gave me the inside scoop on how best to facilitate my work that required assistance from host country officials.

"You are like my sister," one of my local staff told me one day. "That's why I want to let you know something that would benefit you."

"What is it?" I cautiously asked her.

"Stop wearing your purse across your body when you go to meetings outside of the embassy. You are a 'madame, a boss woman'— not a teenager. The folks at the Ministry of Telecommunication like you very much, but you can get more cooperation from them if you look more diplomatic."

What an eye-opener, but it was the truth. While no one could argue that my dress and mannerisms were not tip-top professional, I did have a few habits, like wearing my purse across my body, that were not accepted as professional in other cultures. That staff was a part of the family I created within my section. She took care of me.

I eventually realized that spending so much time laying the foundation for my personal relationships strengthened my professional relationships. The work I did was fundamental to the mission—without communications up and running, the embassy would be disconnected from Washington and the rest of the world.

It was one of the highest priorities, and since most of my team consisted of foreign nationals and American men, it was imperative that we got along, they respected me as a female leader, and I led them as a cohesive unit—a family. We had to trust each other to follow up with our agreed-upon plan. We depended on each other for feedback, smiles, encouragement, and a helping hand. We had to maintain a level of respect and cooperation—just like family. I had only two assignments where the family concept did not go over well, mainly among my American subordinates, but you know what? The work got done in spite of it.

As I've said before, the Foreign Service is more than a job—it's a lifestyle. Once I acclimated, I knew it was my calling. I'm not sure it was Andrew's.

I've refrained from really discussing the closest family to me, Andrew. While I believe that I was the best mother I could be, I have lingering doubts about whether I did enough to give him what he needed to succeed in life. He was an easy child to raise, never a bother to me or others. But boy, oh boy, he made up for it in college and throughout his 20s and early 30s. He found trouble at every corner. Alcohol, marijuana, bad friends, and partying became the norm for this Ivy League boarding school kid. No matter that he had talked to Chelsea Clinton, played with US Marines, roomed with George Foreman's son, dined with President Carter and his family as well as scholars from around the world, lived in seven countries on four different continents, and was admired by ambassadors. Andrew was probably exposed to a life that most people can't even imagine. I assumed with the laying of a great foundation for him, he was destined to be a responsible citizen with a great career. He certainly had the intelligence and personality for it. But my hopes shattered when he went to jail the first time.

The second time he went to jail, I knew that any dreams he had for himself to be responsible and professional were over. The third time he went to jail, I knew that he would have to work hard to just survive in life.

But I never stopped loving and praying for him, not to this very second. It took years, but he finally grew into a responsible man and the most loving, caring father. His past sometimes gets in the way of his present and future, but his determination keeps him moving forward, finding a way to overcome. Watching him work through his difficulties makes me so proud of him. I often smile within as I prod him along and silently say, *That's my boy; he is learning the hard way just like his mom, but he will be all right one day!*

And one more thing about Andrew: After telling me during a drunken rage that I would never see any grandchildren because he was going away and would never be in touch, he has blessed me more than he knows by fathering my grandbabies Keegan, Ian, and Anah. The devil is a liar!

I recall when Andrew met Shaka. They went out to discuss, man to man, our pending marriage. A senior in high school, Andrew made it clear that Shaka better treat me right, or else he'd have to answer to him. It was a mature gesture on Andrew's part and a display of how loyal he is to his mother.

And Shaka, my sweet darling Shaka. I couldn't have cared less to ever find another husband after what Tim and Tommie put me through. I am shocked that I remarried and stunned that I married an African man. Shaka could offer only love and a promise to stand by me through thick and thin. I wasn't sure the guy was serious, so in the process of becoming serious, I told him bluntly that he had to fit into my world—that I would never be able to fit into his. He was fine with that. I had no plans to stay in a foreign country beyond visiting or working, and I couldn't be stressed out by someone pressuring me to do so. At the beginning, I had considered him a nice guy to tease, but when he went to his African grandmother for her opinion and blessing to pursue me as a wife, I knew he was my man. He included family in his decision in choosing a wife, and that touched me.

Shaka and I met when I was assigned to the embassy from 1996 to 1998 in Dar es Salaam, Tanzania, where he worked at Rickshaw Travels at the Sheraton Hotel downtown. He was a kind person, but not my type—or so I thought. When I left for Beirut, we did not keep in touch much. A passing thing, I thought.

Then in September 2000, when we were both assigned to temporary duty in Arusha, Tanzania, where I was assisting with President Clinton's trip for meetings with Burundi's 19 political parties, we reconnected. It was strange to see him again in an unexpected place.

"What a pleasant surprise, Bwana Shaka," I said. "Nice to see you again. Let's get together before the event is over, OK?" I spoke quickly, as my attention was on the tall, mysterious charcoal men from Burundi who hung out in the hotel restaurant and lobby in between supporting their president for the meetings. They intrigued me because they looked African and exotic. Shaka was skinny and light-skinned and wore big glasses. Nerdy! He was nice looking, but had no flare like the Burundians.

Nevertheless, I did not dismiss Shaka altogether. Between the duties of my job, I flirted, getting to know him more. When I got tired of working, I flopped down in the chair at his American Express Travel Services desk in the lobby. I learned that he had been temporarily transferred from Dar es Salaam to Arusha to oversee the Legita Travel Agency's American Express Services division. The embassy in Dar es Salaam employed his services to manage travel for President Clinton's entourage for the Burundi event in Arusha—a plus in my book. Looking better, yes, looking better!

He joked that he was struggling to keep women away from him that week. "Hmm, is that why a smile comes on your face each time I sit here?" I said to him while looking at the lobby bar where the Burundian men had started to congregate again. I did not hear his response in my haste to get to the bar to talk to others.

As I moved throughout the hotel during the day and the lounge at night meeting folks, I would feel those big eyes of his piercing me. We never got truly close on that visit; however, we did exchange numbers and email addresses and a few comments to know this wasn't the end of us. Long emails and phone calls commenced. One thing led to another. Visits between Tanzania and Uganda (where I was then assigned) began. To impress me, one weekend Shaka brought 500 roses with him from Arusha to Kampala—big, beautiful red and white buds. My house looked like a wedding or funeral was about to take place, and it smelled heavenly, like a flower shop. My brother Ryan happened to be visiting me that weekend, and he laughs about it to this day.

We finally said, "I do, and I will" at the altar. After over 15 years of being single, I was married once again, but this time to an African man. He was now family.

In the last years of my service and as a recruiter a few years back talking with young diplomats and prospective diplomats, if I sensed a loneliness or fear of leaving family and friends to work abroad, I would mention support resources the Foreign Service has to help diplomats adapt more easily and quickly. I would share how I managed to keep relationships at home and abroad healthy and lasting. I would tell them that locals, who can make your assignment easy or difficult, will go the extra mile beyond their job description if they sense realness—a connection, a family vibe. Call it family or friendship, but they will work their buns off when they feel that loyalty.

Look for love, support, respect, and honesty, I say. When you find them, you find family and friends. With them, you will be able to make it anywhere—domestic or abroad!

CHAPTER 8

Faith

*"And Jesus answering saith unto them, Have faith in God.
For verily I say unto you, That whosoever shall say unto this
mountain, Be thou removed, and be thou cast into the sea;
and shall not doubt in his heart, but shall believe that those
things which he saith shall come to pass; he shall have
whatsoever he saith.
Therefore, I say unto you, What things so ever ye desire, when
ye pray, believe that ye receive them, and ye shall have them.
And when ye stand praying, forgive, if ye have ought
against any; that your Father also which is in heaven may
forgive you your trespasses.
But if ye do not forgive, neither will your Father which is in
heaven forgive your trespasses."*
Mark 11: 22–26

My seeds of faith in God were planted in a wooden, rundown
house that, when I look at the only picture we have of it,
it brings tears to my eyes. I was 2 years old when the picture
was taken. The date inscribed on it is 1962. My mom is in the
picture wearing raggedy clothes, picking up sticks from the yard
on a cold winter day.

In hindsight, I believe that our home was a place where the junk of more affluent families ended up. The house had gapped plank boards butted together and nailed in place. No insulation. Nothing between floorboards and the dirt crawl space underneath. When the sun was high, light streamed through the cracks, slanted as if we had covered the walls with blinds. We walked on a board propped like a gangway to the back door; warped boards served as stairs to the front door. Our wooden outhouse was in the corner of the backyard, complete with wooden toilet.

I didn't know things could be different, but Momma did. I'd hear her pray to God for help. It was hard to make out most of what she said, but I always heard the words *God, Jesus, help us, my children, money, deliver us*, and *thank you*. Those words were enough to make a small child like me know that things weren't as they should be. I paid no deep attention to her prayers because from what I learned in my teaching in Sunday school, if you called on God, He would answer you. So, Momma had it covered in her prayers. I had no worries with a praying momma like Martha Rae.

Praying was a part of Momma's daily routine—praying and singing old spiritual hymns. Naturally I started praying, too, especially when I headed to the outhouse. I hated going out there, but I had to. In the summer, I'd be watching for snakes stretched out in the tall grass beside the outer walls. In the winter, the cold whistled through, slapping the loosely latched door against its frame and leaving me to shiver all over. *Oh Lord, don't leave me now*, I'd pray. *Jesus, please make this quick and keep the snakes away. Help us to move the toilet closer or inside the house.* I knew no better.

All our praying paid off. I was around 8 years old when we finally moved up in the world. Momma played a local form of the modern-day lottery back then. It was simply referred to as "The Numbers." The story goes that one day she gave her numbers to my big brother Steven to find the local bookie, who was somewhere in the community. Steven jumped on Nancy, our huge family horse, and galloped all over the neighborhood to find him. It was worth him pushing ol' Nancy to her limits because Momma hit it big! Her numbers came up and she put her winnings to good use by hiring a cousin who was a carpenter to build us a home.

Our new home was luxurious compared to where we came from: three bedrooms with closets and beds, a nice kitchen and a separate eating area, a living room, and a family area. We even had a screened-in front porch. Finally, we had a real home just like most of the others in the community. No more teasing from bullies on the bus about living in a shack.

Momma held a housewarming party, and Aunt Lucille, Aunt Hannah, Uncle Jake, and their families came from Florida to celebrate with us. Aunt Inez, who lived down the street from us, was Momma's right hand in coordinating the party. Neighbors and friends from Holmestown came, too. Momma and Daddy even had a DJ on-site. We danced and drank, with plenty excess, so I was told. I vaguely remember the party, but I do remember the hype building up to it. Lots of cooking, decorating, and laughter by everyone. I felt like we had arrived.

That house stood for something, and after all these years, it continues to signify "faith and family." The housewarming started our annual Way family reunion; we celebrated 50 years in 2018. Every year when our family history is read, Momma just beams when the story of the house and party is mentioned. Momma prayed, and she believed—she had faith. Her prayers were answered in a very real and tangible fashion. God answered, just like they taught us in Sunday school. With that chunk of history on faith and my family, I could not go wrong if I kept those values.

I am proud to be the child of God-fearing parents, and while it seems unchristian-like, I do believe that winning from a gambling game was a prayer answered and a blessing from God for my family—a blessing given because Momma prayed for it.

Having this testimony of faith led me to search the Bible for strength and encouragement through my rough and uncertain times. One time when I was on the Greyhound bus going back to college at Albany State, I was depressed and uncertain about my future. Momma had torn an extra hole in me for goofing off at school. I was not being challenged and was thinking about doing something different with my life—like marriage to Andre, my military boyfriend. A lady sitting beside me on the bus noticed I was in deep thought, so she started talking to me. She mentioned Mark, Chapter 11, so I pulled out my Bible and flipped to the passage. Amazingly, it lifted my spirit and gave me hope. I read it again after she fell asleep on the long bus ride. I'm still reading it. It became the basis for keeping my spirit and faith strong. I've worn that page thin in several Bibles through the years. All these years later, I am still thankful to the lady who guided me to that scripture.

I have traveled the world, and when I came home for visits, I ensured I came with gifts and things that showed my success. I rarely spoke of my work, and that led some of the more educated in my family and the community to believe I was goofing off and living a sinful life high on the hog. Little did they know that I was strongest in my faith while overseas. As the Reverend Abe Solomon, a pastor in my church years ago, said, "Take the

Lord with you, baby, and everything will be all right." I took the Lord with me everywhere I went, and because of it, God has masterfully led me through all the pivotal moments in my life.

Early in my career while serving in Guatemala, I was driving home after working late. It had been a long day filled with exploring a complicated communications system that we had just installed. I was an enthusiast and perfectionist in the office, as well as the boss, and wanted to master it before others on my team did, so I worked over the weekend when the embassy was closed. Leaving later that evening after the sun had set, I drove away, my mind filled with my work and with what I wanted to do with Andrew the next day to make up for our missed Saturday.

Bam! Wham! Out of nowhere, just as I pulled into the street behind the embassy, a big car slammed into the side of my shiny new Nissan Sentra at full force. As if in slow motion, my car went flying with me still strapped inside. It hit a wall and bounced over, flipping right-side up and landing with a thud on all four wheels.

Was this really happening to me? I was paralyzed. I couldn't move my hands from the steering wheel. I sat there, staring ahead and feeling the cool breeze from the front of my car where my windshield once was. There was eerie silence, a small tinkle of glass falling to the paved road and steam hissing from both vehicles' punctured and ripped hoses.

Somehow, I managed to use my embassy radio with the help of a witness. "Help! This is Vella, and I was just in an accident behind the embassy; please come!" I managed to get out of my mouth.

The marine on the other end of the radio told me to stay put; help was on the way. They arrived, removed me from the car, and rushed me to the hospital. On the way, I laid in the arms of one of the marines. He was holding me like a baby. He rubbed my shoulder. "You will be fine," he said. *Wow, I always wanted to be held by a U.S. Marine, but just not under these conditions.*

Mark, Chapter 11 came to mind. Being held by that that brave and handsome marine distracted me a lot, but I knew I needed to focus on God more than ever now. *Have faith, have faith, pray, pray, forgive, forgive.*

After a thorough exam in the emergency room, I was given a clean bill of health and allowed to go home within 24 hours of being taken there. The doctors and policemen marveled that I was alive, much less untouched. I spent the next few days in a haze, shaken by what had happened and deeply grateful to God for what had not. Friends and colleagues, including the ambassador to Guatemala at the time, stopped by my house to check on me. "You are truly blessed," they said.

Weeks later when I saw the car, I knew that I was blessed. I couldn't bear the thought of what might have happened to Andrew if I had died. *But why was I spared?* I wondered. *Why me? Why not now? What did God need for me to accomplish while still here on earth before taking me to heaven?* I wracked my brain trying to figure out what my purpose was on earth. I felt burdened and intimidated by the awesome responsibility of those questions. They weighed heavy on my shoulders.

At the time, I had no answers, but I did have a revelation: I could get killed in this profession. It made me realize that I needed to keep faith close to me always.

I sat for months afterward trying to figure out what my purpose in life was—why God spared me that night. Nothing seemed to materialize in my head, and it bothered me that after such a horrific accident, I couldn't find my purpose. Finally, I stopped searching for a response and just lived, but this time with a passion for everything I did. I figured that my reason for still being on earth after such a horrifying experience in my life would be revealed when God was ready to show me.

I was spared a second time in Tanzania when the embassy blew up around me. Amid so much destruction and evil on that August day in 1998 (which coincidentally was my father's birthday), when some I knew who worked in the same building died, I once again sustained no serious injuries—a few scratches and minor cuts. Even more striking, I was calm and collected. I didn't freak out. In the wrong place at the right time, I found a steely resolve to do my job and restore communications. I felt that I was working with a blindfold on and with a cold heart—I saw or felt nothing except to do what I was trained to do. God was with me, I called his name when I realized the situation I was in, and my faith was my eyes and heart. God guided me through what needed to be done and kept me safe while doing it. I was strong for those around me. Some marveled at how I held up through it all.

Before I left Tanzania, I managed a host of installs to set up temporary operations in the wake of the bomb. Those crucial weeks gave me another new outlook. While I had always cared for my local staff, I noticed a true appreciation for them and the work they did so diligently for the embassy. About the third day after the horrific bombing, it dawned on me that one member of my Tanzanian staff was always present. *Has he gone home since the day of the bombing?* I wondered. *Is he working more hours than I am?* And I knew I was putting in at least 16 hours a day. He was even bandaged up in a few areas from getting hit by debris from the bomb blast; however, he was at the embassy and working hard.

"*Kaka* (*brother* in Swahili), take a day off; you have been through a lot," I said.

"No, *Dada* (*sister*), I am OK," he replied.

"Kaka, do you hear me? Please go home and rest with your family. Go, now!"

"Sister, you have been so kind to us," he continued, "more respectful to us and our culture than any supervisor I have had in my many years of working for the embassy. You have treated us like your family, especially me, so I can't leave you to do both your job and mine in these conditions. I will be here working alongside you until I feel I can't stand any longer," he said.

I was humbled by his words and touched by his loyalty. It was a powerful and revealing statement I will never forget about my time in the Foreign Service. I didn't realize that my interactions with them were being graded and the results were so high. I was truly blessed. I attribute this to my faith. It took me to my first of many African countries and broke barriers the local staff had put up against us Americans. Faith moves mountains, if you believe. I believed and was delivered from the jaws of death on August 7, 1998, followed by overwhelming support from many of my staff. They worked countless hours to help rebuild communications when it would not have been held against them, due to the situation, to not come to work or to work limited hours for a while.

As the world began changing and crises became more frequent, I started seeing more of the same attitude from my staff. Some of it was so impactful, all I could do was fall on my knees at night and thank God for them. For example, in another African country, my embassy radio technician saw me worried about our embassy radio network. It was a Friday, and the embassy was closing in about an hour and would not reopen until Tuesday, since Monday was a local holiday in the country.

"Madame, you do not look happy," he said.

"I am just not satisfied with the occasional scratchy noise heard during the radio test this morning," I said.

"Madame, it will be OK. As I told you earlier today, it is not our radio system, but something the technicians at the Ministry of Telecommunication are aware of and promised to rectify early next week," he said.

"Well, I sure wish there was something we could do on our end to at least minimize the noise in case there is turmoil in the country over the weekend," I said, now scratching my head. I knew the country was not stable, and if something happened and the embassy staff could not effectively use the radio network, I would have to pay the price since I was the Chief of Communications for the embassy.

My technician placed his backpack down on the floor with a smile and said, "Madame, let me see if I can tweak it a little more because I do not like to see you worried, especially going into the weekend. You need to be relaxed and enjoy the break."

"It is OK; please just go home and enjoy your family. You did a lot today and look exhausted," I told the tired technician.

"Yes, I am very tired, but you must know that I and my other colleagues will work ourselves to the bone for you, madame. You are a good boss who treats us with so much respect," he said. "The least I can do is to see if I missed something today when I was troubleshooting the system."

It seemed as if locals found refuge in my unpretentiousness, my firm but fair leadership style, my caring about their professional development. Thus, they worked and went above and beyond for me. And the more that I practiced inclusiveness and generosity toward them, the more I realized how important it was to project and feel this type of camaraderie as I continued my career in the Foreign Service.

At a seminar I attended at the Foreign Service Institute in Arlington, Virginia, some months after I retired, I ran into a local Ugandan man I had hired to work in the radio and telephone section at our embassy in Kampala. After the laughing, hugging, and kissing, he said:

"Madame, you can't believe it. After all these years, we now have an IMO boss who treats us good like you did," he said. "We had given up hope of having another boss like you, *the madame*—so tough but so caring and so giving." He clasped my hands and hugged me again.

"I have missed you through the years. Thank you for hiring and trusting me. I am still around and doing very well at the embassy, thanks to you and your teaching," he said. "I truly miss you and my family misses you, too! My wife often asks about *the madame*. Even my father reminds me sometimes of how I was struggling when I first started working for the embassy and how that nice madame took me under her wings and taught me how an embassy worked and how to do my job very well, the embassy way." He went quiet for a few seconds and shook his head as tears slowly crept into his eyes.

A lump rose in my throat. There was silence for what seemed like forever. Eventually, it was broken by the staff when he said in a low voice, "Your kindness will never be forgotten in Uganda, madame." I was humbled again by profound words from a local staff member. It was then, in the halls of the Foreign Service Institute as a retiree, that I realized the impact I had on my foreign staff, their families, their communities, and maybe even their countries. "Kindness," that single word from his mouth, was what I believed earned me the blessings from God for surviving a nasty car wreck in Guatemala, walking out of a bombed building alive and well in Tanzania, surviving a horrible earthquake in the Philippines, and so many other close brushes with death. My kindness was my reason for being spared. It is my belief that God knows the world needs more of it, and I had a lot to share. Even more so, I believe God knew my faith was strong enough to travel the world without fear. He molded me to withstand the rigors of the world so that I could continue my path, sharing the blessing of kindness while I serve him and my country.

It is my belief that God is generous and in the business of saving lives, families, and friendships. He pours out blessings when needed and even when not asked for. For me personally, I call on him, especially in times of trouble, for my share. After we married and Shaka joined the Foreign Service, his attempts at tenure were waylaid by what I perceived as unfairness. Shaka is a likable guy. He treats everyone he meets with dignity and respect. People are drawn to his warm, genuine personality. We are so much alike. But no matter what he did or how he acted, he was faced with challenges for no good reason. He went above and beyond his responsibilities. He went out of his way to be friendly, to help others. He followed the rules. He enforced the rules. He knew his job and did it well. He gave 120 percent at work. Hell, he even lost weight due to the extra work he was doing. No matter. He had an "X" on his back for being who he was, and an "X" was in the box to not be tenured. The situation my dear husband was in was the prime example why we drew upon our faith as we utilized available resources to correct unfair treatment.

The very same day Shaka received his offer to join the Foreign Service, we decided that I would retire within five years. Unfortunately, as we worked our five-year plan, we never thought he would not be tenured. With what he was experiencing, we had to start thinking differently. I would remain in the Foreign Service until mandatory retirement age, and he would return to be a Foreign Service spouse, if it came down to it. We were a team and would make whatever came our way work for our family. However, not without the two Fs that helped me some years back—faith and fight. We had both, but some days we felt weak and defeated. *How would we face family and friends after all the rejoicing when Shaka joined? Would I really have to work until the mandatory retirement age of 65?* The questions, the doubts. We had them all. We prayed and prayed relentlessly. Shaka's tenure just had to come through.

Despite the uncertainty, I knew it was time for me to leave the Foreign Service at the end of our five-year plan, but I hated to do it if Shaka's career was in jeopardy. We had unfinished personal projects, and we loved the lifestyle. I was frustrated that God wasn't making it easy. It was hard to remember that God is omniscient, even when you can't see past tomorrow.

Faith paid off yet again for us, and Shaka got tenured.

Retiring took a leap of faith, and I think because I leaped and trusted that God would catch us no matter how things worked out, God worked in our favor. I don't think Shaka would have still been in the Foreign Service and with his good name if we hadn't trusted God with the bigger plan.

I'm not usually this open with my faith. I certainly haven't talked about it with others unless they approached me. Yet looking back, I realize how much I depended on it during my years with the Foreign Service. Sometimes, despite our intelligence, strength, best efforts, and preparation, we can't control a situation. We can't predict the outcome. Some people are terrified of this. I've seen senior officers hyperventilate over something as small as a message being sent with a comma instead of a semicolon. I have seen the strong get teary-eyed and shake from fear during a crisis or attack. It truly is hard to predict how you will react in a situation, no matter how much you are trained, but one thing I have always relied on was my faith to get me through times of crisis, both personal and professional. My faith never failed me.

If I faced an uncontrollable situation without my faith, I'd probably hyperventilate or get teary-eyed, too. Let me be clear, however—this is not to say those folks did not have faith. I am saying that *I* would probably be that way if I did not have faith. But I know that I can't control anything—God is in full control. He has my back. He knows what's going to happen. I see myself as a tiny dot on a big, colorful map of the world. I'm small, and that's scary. It is comforting, however, to know God and experience his work firsthand in my life. It does not take the fear away when going through difficult situations, but it sure does provide something to believe in to soothe the heart and keep those wobbly legs moving forward when "good for nothing" comes at you from all directions.

If I've learned anything from growing older, it's that I understand that God's time is not my own. I pray and fully expect him to answer—tomorrow. He may decide that it's best to defer an answer for a month. Or a year. I don't like this one bit, but I've learned that, particularly in my life, he takes a big-picture view. He made me, but his perspective is a little different than mine. And though I don't want to admit it, I've had to bite my tongue, sit myself down, and learn a little patience. I wasn't too good at that.

Neither are applicants vying to be invited into the Foreign Service. They do not like the waiting around to hear something from the Department of State. When it looks like they are about to give up, I tell them one of my faith stories. Hang tight, I say. If you truly want this lifestyle and career path, be patient with the process and don't give up. Part of the process is waiting. It's that way when pursuing a career with the Foreign Service— jumping through application hoops during the screening and hiring process and biding time in between. And it remains that way once you are in: waiting to get assigned, waiting for your medical clearance or security clearance update, waiting for your household effects to be shipped or arrive, waiting to be told when it is safe to go to a certain part of town, waiting for a response from Washington on a curtailment or a medevac . . . wait, wait, wait. This is why faith is so important *to me* and was so important for me in the Foreign Service. I did what I could, and when I couldn't, I waited and trusted God to work it out for me.

My belief makes me whole. In the early-morning hours, when Shaka and the rest of the living world are sleeping, I sneak out of bed into the darkest part of my house to seek God and feel nurtured in his presence. My belief is what connects me to him. I'm not saying that everyone should do as I do; I'm only saying that it's worked for me and still does.

He has given me talents to see me through, and I use them as best I can. I can't do any more than that. Whether it's a hiccup in my well-thought-out plans or a full-blown crisis, I worry, but I do not give in or give up so easily. And especially not before giving God a chance. I just turn it over to him and let him guide me through—success or failure. If it's out of my hands, it's in his; therefore, the results were meant for me, Vella, from the man upstairs—Almighty God!

CHAPTER 9

Regret

*Regret gives us the chance to do things differently if the
opportunity arises again, but would you do it differently the
second time around?*

Regret. We all have it. What matters is what we do with it.
I'm one of those people who has overanalyzed every situation I've found myself in. What possessed me to marry two
different men when I did not even know what love was? Why
couldn't I see the signs of Andrew's drug and alcohol abuse?
Why did I allow folks to run over me in my earlier years in the
Foreign Service?

Asking myself these hard questions over the years has forced
me, in good ways and bad, to confront those things in my
personality in hopes of turning them around. Sometimes, I'm
so embarrassed, disgusted, or tired of my actions that it forces
me to find a better way of dealing with some situations. And
other times, there is no solution, no matter how hard I try to
find one, and I have learned that letting go can be excruciating
but liberating.

Early in my career, as I've said several times before, it took
everything I had within me to open my mouth and contribute

to a conversation. My Southern accent and self-perceived lack of knowledge compared to my colleagues kept me on the sidelines. In meetings, I'd listen to the conversational banter and think, *That idea is not going to work*, but I'd keep my mouth shut. I did not know how to eloquently explain the solution I had in my head, so I didn't speak up. In hindsight, I should have just said it. Seconds, hours, or days later, someone would eventually suggest my exact idea, and I'd kick myself.

It took years for me to step out of my comfort zone, but when I did, I became known as Vella Who Gets Things Done, Vella the Dependable, Vella Who Knows, etc. I didn't become a chatterbox after stepping out of that comfort zone, but if an idea came to mind and was relevant, I said it—not in my head but out loud and in real time. I had a seat at the table, and when I spoke, people listened and respected what I had to say.

It took years to realize that everyone didn't know more than me—in fact, at any given time, we're all just trying to move forward in our careers. It certainly helps move the mission forward when all collaborate, including me. Yes, I truly regret not being a true contributor to change from the beginning of my Foreign Service career.

No telling how far I could have been in my career upon retiring if I was not afraid to speak up in my early years. I had so much to offer in the Foreign Service, but I was a late bloomer, or, should I say, a late contributor. I regret that.

I regret not properly celebrating my success in the Foreign Service. I took the blessings, secretly thanked God, and moved on like it was nothing. To be honest, I loved being successful, but I was also afraid of it. I was afraid that if I tooted my own horn and failed along the way, I would have to return to Holmestown.

That would have been the end of me. I honestly feel that because of this fear, I unconsciously sabotaged great opportunities. I saw opportunities, knew how to seize them, had folks at very high levels in my corner, but sabotaged myself time and time again when I needed to act.

I did not start out in my career seeking career-enhancing assignments. Back then, I would submit my bid for the 15 countries that appealed to me and hope for the best. When I finally started strategically and aggressively seeking assignments instead of hoping for the best, my career accelerated, and I reached the coveted grade of 01. So, I knew what it took to move to the next level, but I was content and genuinely happy moving at my own pace so as not to jeopardize the wonderful career and lifestyle I had. *This was my career and there were many years ahead of me, so why more so quickly—stumbling and running over others in the process?* That was my excuse.

Mid-career, I had a once-in-a-career opportunity to move out of IT to another so-called more prestigious field I had demonstrated proficiency in when acting in that capacity, but I got cold feet. The path was laid out for me; all I had to do was start walking toward the golden opportunity. I really should be ashamed to say that I botched up the opportunity just to remain on the same safe track I was on in the IT field. I knew IT. I was happy with IT. I was progressive within that field. And I was finally well-respected among my peers in the field—women and men. So, why take the risk or have to start all over making a name for myself in a new field? There was no guarantee that I would be truly happy and successful on that side of the track. Now, in hindsight, I think: *Silly me for letting all those self-sabotaging thoughts creep into my head. I could have been bigger, better, and more helpful to my colleagues and country along the way in that position.* I regret that.

I regret not speaking out against discrimination and harassment earlier in my career when I experienced or witnessed them. Most of all, I regret not speaking out later in my career when these forces touched my family—my spouse. In 2010, Shaka became an enthusiastic entrant in the US Department of State Foreign Service. When offered the position in the Foreign Service, it was as if he had won a trillion-dollar jackpot. I knew he would do great things—he was smart, dedicated, and hardworking. Others knew, too. As the spouse of a US diplomat, he had been performing General Services Office-type work for many years, under many conditions, and excelling along the way. Once he transitioned to the Foreign Service, the major things that changed were his title, security clearance, and pay. Shaka proved himself to be capable, flexible, and by the book, but that wasn't enough for someone who just could not get past the fact that he was an immigrant who had made it into the Foreign Service. The once wonderful post of assignment he enjoyed became a living hell for him. It was noticeable, and he informed me of what he was experiencing every night since I did not accompany him at that assignment. To make a long story short, he was set up not to be tenured, but he did not want to speak out, and asked me not to. Being his wife and an Equal Employment Opportunity counselor, and listening to and seeing what he was enduring, ate at me to my very core. Due to what was happening to Shaka, I postponed my retirement to see how things would turn out. We suffered emotionally and physically. I did not want to believe this had happened to us. However, we continued to perform at our highest levels and kept the usual big smiles on our faces—wishing and praying at night and at church for a miracle to turn the situation around.

Then, while on a tandem assignment in Kabul, Afghanistan, God sent a miracle our way. This miracle was the catalyst that turned things around in a big way for us. Shaka, less than three months away from having to return his Department of State badge signifying his official separation from the Foreign Service, was tenured and promoted despite the campaign against him. We were blessed! We got our miracle, but I still regret not speaking out and not encouraging my husband more to expose the blatant bigotry he endured. Without the revealing information that landed in his lap many months later when he was out of the hostile environment, the outcome may not have been favorable for him or for our future. So, I regret waiting, but I truly believe God had us go through that year-and-a-half-long ordeal to become stronger in our faith, our work, and our relationship.

I have quite a few personal regrets. I regret marrying at such a young age when I did not know the true meaning of love. Granted, we got Andrew out of the deal, but I was just not prepared to take responsibility for two more lives—a husband and a child. I wish I had waited.

I regret not being truthful to my sisters when they hurt me to the core with their actions and words. I do not even know if they knew I was hurting or not. I regard myself as a peaceful, giving, loving person, and the baby sister. So, I never spoke out—never an "ouch, that hurt me" or "that was not nice." Since we were raised close-knit, they were my friends, and I did not want to jeopardize our friendships. So, I endured what they dished out, but at a cost. Peace is what I wanted between us, but it cost me peace within.

I regret not inviting my best friend Heather to my and Shaka's wedding, and was saddened that I was not invited to theirs. When we were both in our mid-20s and I needed her more than I ever have in our friendship, she had given me what I perceived as a serious brush-off, with harsh words that still resonate through me whenever I think of that day. So, I thought she wasn't interested in my life any longer, nor did she want me to be a part of hers. But after bringing it up with her over 30 years later, we worked through our misperceptions. I wish we could have reconciled before so much time and life passed between us.

I regret not confronting someone before they died who I believe did something wrong to me as a little girl. While the person was not blood, they were a part of our family. Knowing what he tried to do to me, he may have tried and been successful in carrying out his dirty habits with other young girls. I truly regret not speaking out, but the last time I saw this person alive, I saw regret in those ugly, dirty eyes, and his filthy hands were shriveled up with pain. I am not sure if I felt sorry for him.

Those are major regrets, but I have two regrets that run deeper than those. First, I deeply regret not spending one Saturday evening with my oldest brother, Douglas, which was the evening he died. I had every opportunity to and did not. In fact, I burden myself with the thought that if I had, he would not have died.

I had come home from college with my roommate, and Douglas, always so proud of me, wanted to take me and my friend to the officers' club on base at Fort Stewart, Georgia, where he was assigned. I knew he wanted to show us off to his friends so he could say, "Hands off, get back," when they tried to get close to us. Douglas was personable, but he did not take crap from anyone. He fought and drank, but he was smart—an officer in the United States Army. He had acted like this when going out with us before. That is what big brothers do, I supposed. However, for two young college women with hormones raging, it is not what we needed, and especially not that night since we had a gruesome week studying for our final exams. The previous times Douglas had taken us to the officers' club weren't fun for us. We were ready to bust loose on the dance floor of Fort Stewart's enlisted men's club instead. The club was called "the Zoo." It was naughty and wild, and we loved being in the thick of it.

I told Douglas that it sounded like a plan—until something better came along, that is. Earlier in the day while in town, a few young GIs had caught our eyes and asked us out. I remember passing Douglas' house early that Saturday evening in a playful mood with my college friend on the way to the Zoo to meet up with our new GI friends. I never called to tell Douglas that our plans had changed. *I'll ask for forgiveness the next day,* I thought to myself. What a horrible baby sister I was. That next day, a Sunday, I did not even call or stop by his house to explain why we did not show up to go out with him and to tell him that we were headed back to the college. We thought it was cute and that he would understand. After all, I was his favorite sister, and he would forgive me.

That next week, back at college, I awoke one night from a terrible dream. Our family was caught in the middle of a heated military battle, and soldiers were everywhere with long rifles in their hands. The gunshots sent us scrambling, with Douglas running behind everyone in our family. "Don't look back! Keep running!" he said.

I heard a gunshot louder than the other shots. I looked back as Douglas slumped to the ground.

"Keep running, Vella Jane! Go! Go!" he yelled.

More gunshots in my dream, and then a knock at my college dormitory door.

The sleepy-eyed neighbor said there was a phone call for me on the shared hallway phone. It was my mother.

Momma said that rather than coming home with my friend Heather, as I usually did, I was to ride home with my sisters Rachel and Emma and Emma's husband, Carl, who were going to be in town that afternoon. I wasn't sure what was going on, but it seemed plausible. Early that afternoon, after my exams, I piled into the back seat between Emma and Rachel, with my little suitcase in my lap. Final exams were over. I could breathe lighter. I was ready for some fun at the Zoo, but not until I made things right with Douglas. I was going to hang out with him that weekend.

For that group of girls, the car was quiet. *Why?* I wondered. "What's up?" I asked as I looked from one to the other with a giddy smile on my face.

"Douglas was sick," Emma said. She looked away. Rachel turned her head toward the window.

"He's fine, now," Emma said, looking weary and dazed. "He is OK now."

My brother-in-law, Carl, started speeding while looking at me in his rearview mirror. Rachel suddenly started sniffling, and I knew she did not have a cold. I could not see her face, since now her body was twisted toward the window.

"OK, what's really going on?" I asked timidly.

In unison, they turned to me: "Douglas is dead, Jane."

Disbelief rolled through my body. I started screaming and shaking uncontrollably.

Douglas! No! No! No!

The weekend prior, while my friend and I were out having a good time with GIs, my brother was home struggling for his life. Oh, God, I did not know. His wife said he went to sleep in the early evening hours and never woke up, but she did hear him grumbling in his sleep. I wonder if he was fussing at me or telling God to take care of his baby sister. I have no idea and never will. What I know for absolute is that I didn't get to tell Douglas that I appreciated his gesture, but I had a real date. "I love you, Big Bro" is what I also would have told him, because his face lit up whenever I told him that.

I regret this deeply, and because of it, I try to never leave when visiting home without trying to be with my parents and every sibling I can find, if only for a second or two. I tried to explain this to my sister Brittany recently during a venting conversation when she complained that I once came home, and we were to do something together, but I cut it short to visit my other siblings. She wasn't buying it, and I suppose that unless she experienced what I did with Douglas' death, I am not sure if she, or anyone else, would ever understand that after Douglas' death, I had to divide my time with all immediate family members, and not just a few, when I visited from abroad.

As much as not saying goodbye to Douglas hurt, my other deepest regret hurts more. I regret temporarily losing Andrew to drugs and alcohol, and seeing him incarcerated and in rehab. I believe I made a lot of mistakes; even Brittany and Momma tell me that I made mistakes in raising my son. Because I was not in a normal career or lifestyle, I had to make a lot of hard decisions based on what would be best for my son.

I sent him with his Aunt Rachel to Georgia when he was still a baby because I knew she knew best how to handle an infant—and a premature one like my sweet baby boy. I was having major trouble in my marriage and had a stressful job I could not afford to lose, so Rachel agreed to help me out until I came home in a few months to get him. By then, my baby boy would have developed more, and I would be physically and emotionally stronger to care for him. That was a tough but wise decision to save my life and my son's.

Then, when he was not even 5 years old, my career kicked off. I packed our bags and started our new life in different countries in the Foreign Service. Still, it was important to me and to him to know family. At least once a year after I joined the Foreign Service, I had him spend time in Georgia when his school in the country I was assigned to was on summer break. Brittany used to send her kids home from New York for the summer, too. It was the norm in the family. Sometimes, I flew home with him to Georgia, and other times when I could not take leave, he was escorted by airline attendants. Regardless of how he got home to Georgia, giving him the opportunity to get to know and enjoy his grandparents and other family members on both parents' sides was my intent. I did not see harm in that. He always came back to me with lots of stories to tell that made me laugh.

As he grew older, I wanted him to expand his horizons to have more opportunities later in life. So, I sent him to boarding school for junior high and high school. As well-behaved as Andrew was when I decided to send him and his cousin Virginia to boarding school, I never imagined I was doing something wrong.

And yet for everything I felt I was doing right for Andrew, there was nothing I could do to outwit his DNA. His father had struggled with some of the same vices, and, like it or not, my son was born with a proclivity to do the same. The signs were there, but I could not see them in time to help him.

Ethel, his nanny and our house lady in Africa, said she found cigarettes in the house during a time Andrew visited from boarding school. My daddy told me that he thought he saw Andrew with a cigarette in his hand at the edge of the yard one day when he was visiting them from college. My siblings made subtle remarks about his sometimes odd behavior or about him hanging out with his Uncle Ronald and his dubious friends when he was home from college and I was overseas. I did not see it. I had taught Andrew right from wrong, including telling him to never, ever use drugs or drink—he knew better. Nevertheless, each time someone came to me about the topic and my son, I asked him if it was true. "Mom, I do not know why they are storying on me," he'd say. "Are you going to believe them or your son?" He knew I loved him to the moon and back, and he knew what to say to throw me off track.

If we were physically together, I would hug him and say, "Son, alcohol and drugs will make you crazy and destroy your life, so continue to stay away from them, please."

"I know that, Mom, and I will never use any of that stuff. I am smarter than that!" he would reply. He looked me dead in my eyes with those puppy dog eyes and denied it. I trusted him, so I simply did not take the stories I heard as seriously as needed.

No, not my child, I thought. Boy, was I wrong.

I finally believed it when I approached him about it yet again, and he told me out of his own mouth that it was true.

So, when he called me one day and said he was going to jail, it should not have been a surprise, even though it was. After about nine months locked up, he spent a year in rehab to get his life together, but it didn't help him. He wasn't ready. The following two years, he was in and out of jail, colleges, and relationships. Hell, I even sent him to Africa to spend some time with his stepfather's family to separate him from the vices of America. It did not help!

It was hard on me seeing him in jail. I figured he would realize the error of his ways and change, so there was some consolation there while he was locked up. What I was not prepared for was checking him into rehab. That was serious business. It meant that he had an illness. He was an alcoholic and he used drugs—double death if not treated by God himself. It was in his DNA on both sides of the family, so I should have known that man could not change him, only prayer, time, and God. My child, my sweet baby boy!

Why did God select my son to be consumed by those vices?

What did I do wrong?

How could I have stopped it?

What could I have done differently, and would it have been better for him?

What hurts me to the core about it all is that Andrew, to this day, tells me that I was and still am the best mom anyone could ask for, and he made the bad choices himself, not me.

Still, I carry the burden of regret!

Thank God for Shaka, because he helped me get through those dark years, and I mean very dark years, as Andrew "lived" his life. When Shaka came into the bedroom and saw me curled up in a knot with red eyes after speaking to someone from home, he would say, "Vella, it's going to be all right, baby." During deep conversations between him and me about Andrew, Shaka would tell me: "Vella, you did nothing wrong. It is Andrew's path. Everybody has a path from God, and all the crying in the world cannot change it, so accept it and just be there for him through his journey." He would say that each time, and believe it or not, it decreased the pain.

The regret and pain associated with Andrew's struggle lingers with me to this very day, but at least it doesn't hurt like it did back then. I share my experience with Andrew and his path with other parents who approach me about what they are going through with their children. And you know what? It is always a child who has had the world and the best of opportunities laid out before them.

Regret. We can't get around it. In retrospect, it has made me wiser and stronger, and more caring, cautious, grateful, understanding, compassionate, God-fearing, faithful, and loving.

I have these words of wisdom to pass on to anyone about feeling regret for anything in their personal or professional life: When you feel regret, instead of feeling bad or like a failure, turn it into a success by using the experience to guide others in similar situations. It eases the pain!

CHAPTER 10

Forgiveness

"And when you stand praying, if you hold anything against anyone, forgive them, so that your Father in heaven may forgive you your sins."
Mark 11:25

Here's what I know about forgiveness: It's hard to do. I should know. I've had plenty of practice trying to forgive people at various times in my life.

I'll start with the hardest first. For years, I played by the rules in the Foreign Service. As one of the few African-Americans *and* women in the IT and communications field, I possibly was a token, but I also knew I was a role model. I considered it a privilege to serve my country and worked as hard as I could to be a worthy representative of women and African-Americans—not only for those in our country, but also for those in other countries who had never interacted with a woman or African-American in a professional role. I recognized that many women around the world couldn't imagine doing something like I was doing simply because of their gender or race—it was unprecedented or taboo in their culture.

I advocated for everything the Foreign Service stood for, and when colleagues had issues, I encouraged them to work within the system, to follow the rules. Give the process a chance—it won't let you down, I'd say.

I received awesome performance evaluations and many awards and commendations throughout my career. I did my work, did it well, and was recognized. If a suggestion was made that sounded doable, I made it a personal mission to bring it to fruition. I paid close attention to those in upper management—their work habits, how they spoke to others, how they handled conflicts, and even how they dressed. I sought mentors who could advise me both professionally and personally. I modeled my work ethic after those who knew how to get things done and were kind to others in the process.

I was also proud of working for the Department of State. In Holmestown, I held my head high, pretending not to notice the stares from folks when I walked by. "That's Martha Rae and Eugene's baby daughter. She's a diplomat or something like that," I'd hear them whisper. My family became small-town celebrities because of the career I chose, and the money and presents I sent from around the world added to the mystique.

Had I not believed so blindly in the collective mission of the Foreign Service, I might not have been blindsided when my security clearance was suspended. I was a solid and honest part of the team, working to promote the sitting US president's foreign policy agenda for the country assigned and to provide services to US citizens abroad. I was a team player, followed the rules, went above and beyond, never swayed, never let personal business cloud my judgement.

Out of the blue, I was escorted out of the embassy in Cameroon, in front of customers and staff—with no explanation—and allowed to take only my purse with me. All that was missing was a swift kick on my rear end to break me down like a useless dog! I was humiliated. My face flushed, my legs wobbling, not sure what was happening to me. *What did I miss? How could this have happened with no warning? Not me! Not do-every-thing-right Vella.* I always crossed my t's and dotted my i's. When I was walking in the blistering heat to my car, I did a quick replay of my time in the Foreign Service, but nothing came to mind that would warrant me being ushered out of the embassy. *What could have brought this type of havoc into my life?* was my thought as I drove home, bewildered, with salty stinging tears in my eyes.

I was deeply hurt. I felt betrayed and abandoned.

When the air cleared, and the legal wrangling was over, I received a letter advising that my security clearance was reinstated. Just like that.

As suddenly as they suspended my clearance, they reinstated it. Wow, that was one of those deals where the average person would either have just left the Foreign Service or sued. Not me. It was nearly impossible, but I had refused to allow people to see me quiver during the ordeal. Finally, I was getting back on my feet. It felt supernatural. I prevailed. I forgave, I survived. I moved on.

I forgave anyone and everyone who had a hand in the suspension. I'd never experienced divine intervention so direct and complete, except from what I know of my momma hitting the numbers to build our new house or when I was on my knees praying when I received the call from the Department of State offering me a career. But that's what it was, because there was no way I could have forgiven on my own.

I learned some important lessons. I realized that the Foreign Service is not perfect. Like every other organization or corporation, it is full of bureaucracy, and people sometimes become misguided about the mission.

I discovered that moving on to the next level is impossible until what's hurting me is out and done. I loved my career. Holding grudges would only hurt me professionally and decrease my lifespan due to the stress. Don't try to suppress your feelings. Deal with them, or that hatred will eat you inside out. If all else fails, move on and forget it.

And I did. It's ironic that I worked as a recruiter for the Foreign Service while waiting to learn the fate of my career, but never once did I let on that anything was amiss. I meant it and still do when I tell people that the Foreign Service is a great career. I don't think I would have felt that way if I hadn't had the blessing of forgiveness within me.

At the other end of the spectrum, it was easy to forgive my son's father. He was the father of my child, and that is why I went to Pastor Williamson, the pastor of my church at the time, for prayer and guidance. I second-guessed myself about leaving him, but I knew he wouldn't change. He made promises he couldn't keep. He still does.

But we were young, and he also did not know what love or being a husband meant. We were both young and caught up. We labeled all the wrong things as love, but when we got married, we realized we were wrong—they were not love. Why hate him when he was not mature enough to be married and be a father? After I spoke with my pastor and prayed one more prayer about the situation, I knew what I had to do. I was at peace with it from that moment on. I forgave him, and I am glad that I knew that forgiveness doesn't cover someone's shortcomings; it only keeps you from being trapped in them. It frees you from their control. I divorced him and was free!

———————

I've exhausted myself thinking about why Tommie, my second husband, came into my life. I was a bit jaded and still did not know what love was about, but being a single mother with a young child, I thought I needed a man to take care of me and my child. That's a mistake I'll never make again.

My fiasco with Tommie made me realize that sometimes you must get hurt so other people can feel whole or complete. He had big plans but no gumption to see them through. He couldn't see around obstacles, and once he got frustrated, he tried his best to take everything in sight downhill with him.

Once my son and I left for my first post of assignment in the Philippines, I thought that I left that relationship in the past, never to think of him again. I didn't need a man. I had God and a lot of new friends. It's a good thing, because Andrew, now older, divulged that Tommie would sometimes fuss at him for no reason at all after I left for work.

The rage almost got the better of me, and Tommie was lucky that I was across the ocean. Had I been just down the street, I would have done him in with a baseball bat—seriously!

Over 30 years later, I have not totally forgiven Tommie. It's a work in progress, and I am almost there. I do know that if I don't let it go, I will remain weighed down in that little corner of my heart. There is a levity to forgiving. It makes me feel lighter, and I need this piece of weight to drop so I can feel like a falcon. One day I will make my way to his hometown in Louisiana to find and speak with him—without my baseball bat. I truly believe that's what I need to do to totally forgive him for being a coward and leaving me in the middle of the night—no note, just an empty closet and my son left behind at the babysitter's.

And then there are those who have forgiven me. Being forgiven feels the same way—lighter. I've asked Shaka for forgiveness for getting upset when his family asks for "wants." We have given generously to them for necessities and some "wants" since I met him, but at one point their "wants" increased. It was at a time when we were struggling to meet our needs. Times were rough for us. We told them, but it seemed as if they thought we were joking. To them, we Americans, and American diplomats at that, had a lot of money. It seemed as if they judged us as wealthy by the spending we did on vacation when we visited, not knowing that we started saving right after the last trip for the current trip.

When telling them things were not as rosy for us as they imagined just wasn't enough to make them realize we were not rich, we needed a different strategy. So we saved and brought his parents to the States for a visit—the first time they had ever been to the United States of America. Wrong move, in my opinion. We bought them things to make them happy, so again, all they saw was us spending. Silently, I became even more frustrated. My dear sweet mother-in-law picked up things and said, "I want this," but she never looked at the price tag unless I drew her attention to it. Then, she would say, "I see the price, but I still want it. My children are US diplomats. They can afford it." I was so stressed during their visit. I wanted them to have a great time and get what they wanted, but we just could not afford it all.

Shaka understood my stress but was deeply offended that I complained so much about his parents to him. I felt so ashamed about it because he should have been able to get his parents whatever they wanted since he was working, too. However, I felt that Shaka should spend money on his family within reason, and only after the needs of his little family—and some of his wife's (my) "wants"—were met. I didn't think of it as putting them second, but he left their house and married me and made a promise to God to take care of me.

A cultural difference I had to come to grips with is that I can tell my parents, "No, I can't afford that for you," or "You really do not need that," whereas it's taboo in the African culture to tell your parents that when you have supposedly made it big. Well, when it came to my pocket and our livelihood, I had to put culture to the side and say no, and convince Shaka it should be no. "Maybe another time, but no for now," I'd say. He didn't like it back then, even though he told me he understood. Knowing my darling Shaka, saying he "understood" was forgiveness. I accepted it any way he gave it to me, because each time I had to put my foot down, it weighed my heart down.

Not everything one feels guilty of or bad about will be resolved with the wonderful three words we pray for, *"I forgive you."* I've asked Andrew for forgiveness for something I am not sure I needed forgiveness for, but I did anyhow because I felt weighed down about it. Did I fail him? I believe I did, but not due to neglect or selfish reasons. I dragged him around the world fulfilling my dream and believed it would be a win for me and him. I got to travel, and he benefited from getting a great education and personal exposure to the world. I thought it was awesome, but I didn't see his vulnerabilities when I sent him to boarding school. Had he stayed with me until he went off to college, I could have prevented him from spiraling into a path of self-destruction and eventually several stints of incarceration—I think. How could I have let that happen to the one person I love more than life itself?

Through the years when Andrew was having issues, I heard family and friends share, implicit and implied, so many reasons as to why he was doing what he did with no regard for himself or his family. I would rather have had moral support instead of their theories. The career I fell into did not allow me to raise my child as a typical child in the United States, but they critiqued him as if he were *typical*. It was not fair, but I could not make them see it. So, I listened, I smiled with my head hung down, and I hurt—silently. Little did they know that I also prayed to God to place angels around my child to substitute for family support.

God came through for me because Andrew has been through some tough and rough stuff, and he is still standing. Despite his resiliency, I feel, even up to this day, like a failed mother. Yet, I keep loving him while he works his way through the obstacles God places in his path to test his faith. Friends and family were mean and nasty, but through it all, I kept talking to my son about change and praying to God to keep him alive and well through it all. Andrew heard me, and so did God. Andrew is alive and well today with real-life experience to share with others, including his own children.

On numerous occasions I have asked Andrew to forgive me. Yet, he consistently says there is nothing to forgive. He tells me: "Mom, I did what I wanted to do even though I heard you repeatedly telling me how destructive it was." *Why did he do this to himself, why did he do it to me?* Not everything has a clear reason or explanation, so I have stopped beating myself up and accepted what my son keeps telling me—stop blaming myself. "Mom, there is nothing to forgive you for because you did nothing wrong; you were and still are a perfect mom!"

———————

As written in this chapter, I do forgive or at least have the intelligence to know that I should forgive. Forgiving sets me free, and as long as I have the right mind to realize that I should forgive, I aim to forgive. As much as I do not forgive or am slow to forgive, God loves and still forgives me because I am a wonderful person molded by him with the spirit of forgiveness in my heart.

CHAPTER 11

Generosity

I did not learn to give. Giving is in my DNA.

Growing up happy and content in our board house before Momma caught the numbers and built a new house, I thought everyone's family used an outside toilet or stuffed the cracks in the walls with old clothes to keep the cold and insects out. When our yard got crowded with leaves or debris, we raked it using twigs like a broom—the same twigs that Momma used to beat us if we acted up. Prior to upgrading to our new home, I recall washing in a tin basin of water, rubbing clothes clean in a tub of suds before hanging them on the clothesline to dry, and eating mostly food we grew.

We had meat for dinner during hog-killing season, or when ol' Mr. Billy down the road, who worked at Friendly Grocery Store, brought us the meat that the butcher deemed not suitable to package and put out for sale. If it didn't look too good, Momma would cut off the bad parts and boil the rest to ensure it was OK to serve her family.

We weren't rich, but I figured we weren't poor, either, by the way Momma and Daddy were always sharing with friends and neighbors—a bag of veggies from our garden, a jug of homemade brew from the smokehouse, a handmade quilt Momma made herself, and sometimes even money if the person asking was desperate.

When we moved into our new house, the spirit of giving increased. Because God had blessed us with a new house and furnishings, I suppose my parents felt it was their responsibility to share. I didn't think twice when I came home from school to discover a less fortunate person stretched out on our couch, taken in by my parents when they had no place else to go. It wasn't uncommon to see a distant cousin named "Butch" from down the road raking our yard out of gratitude for my parents giving him some pocket change or a temporary place to stay. Momma didn't bat an eyelash at fixing a hot meal or giving away a piece of bread to someone who asked for something to eat.

What touched me the most was how she would sit on the porch cutting rags to hand-stitch quilts to give away. She never expected anything in return. Days or even weeks later, after a quilt was finished and delivered, the recipient would stop by with a little something for the family to say thank you. I can still see Mr. Harry Lee walking home, carrying several quilts for his family before winter set in. When it turned cold, he reminded Momma how thankful he and his wife, Ms. Nelda, were for the quilts that kept them and their children warm in their old wooden house, similar to our old house. Making those quilts was a God-given talent, and Momma was generous with what she did with that talent.

Momma was always harping on us about gratefulness and helping the destitute. Hearing her talk, seeing her in action, and listening when people like Mr. Harry Lee stopped by became defining moments in my life. I, too, wanted to be generous. It made me feel proud knowing I was a part of helping someone else feel or do better.

Daddy shared, too. He might have drunk himself almost to the bottom of the bottle, but he'd offer Mr. Felix Brown, Mr. Mack Jones, Cousin Farrell, Uncle Charlie, and anyone who shared his last crack of spirited beverage, even if they did not ask for it. When it came to helping friends, he didn't know how to say no, and there were times when his own family did without because he gave some of his hard-earned money or took out a loan from the Hinesville Bank for a buddy in need. Most of them never paid him back in full or at all; their sad stories only fueled Daddy's need to give them more.

Seeing the generosity around me in those days, I followed my parents' example as best I could, considering I did not have much to be generous with back then. I did charitable things like help others with their homework or fill out a form or application for an older person in the community. I also remember once while in college, my sister Brittany sent me $50. The very day I received it, my roommate told me she wanted to go home that coming long weekend to visit her parents, whom she had not seen in months, but neither she nor her parents had money to fund the trip. I gave her half of the money I had just received so she could buy a round-trip bus ticket. She did not ask me for it; I offered it to her. I felt so good helping her. When she returned from home with a big smile on her face and some cookies her mom had made for me, I felt great and like the luckiest person in school!

Generosity was in my DNA since way back then, and it extended throughout college and into my professional life. The more I gave, the better I felt, and the more I wanted to give. Folks, including my siblings and friends, called me "too kind," labeled me as a pushover or weak. Some thought I was just plain stupid, but it did not matter. Giving of my time or from my belongings, including my purse, made me feel good deep within. I had the goods and the smarts—and so I gave. Giving was natural, as well as empowering, for me. I didn't have much in my pre-Foreign Service days, but I gave what I could. Hell, when I left for the Foreign Service, I even gave my trailer home and the furnishings in it to my neighbor, whose trailer was worse than mine. Giving someone a home with furnishings when you're in your late 20s is unspeakable. But I did it, and it felt good to my core.

Then I joined the Foreign Service, and my entire perspective about my station in the world changed. Virtually overnight, I went from living in a small trailer home in Plata, Georgia, to having more money than I knew what to do with and living in fancy hotels and houses so big and beautiful I often thought I had died and gone to heaven. I'd send money home to my family and splurge on extravagant things like a nice stereo and haircuts from a real beauty salon instead of from a cousin under the big oak tree in my parents' backyard.

I was living high on the hog, or so I thought, until I realized the socioeconomic backgrounds of some of my fellow new Foreign Service colleagues. It opened my eyes to the extreme wealth in the world. I never realized that people paid as much to get a haircut as it cost to feed my entire family for a few days, drove cars the richest person in Holmestown could not afford to even think about owning, and threw out food they called "leftovers" when it was perfectly fine. Lord have mercy, these people had live-in maids.

The contrast was maddening. At times when I became overwhelmed by it all, I grew reserved and confused, hesitant to share my meager background with colleagues and scared to share my new lifestyle with family and old friends back home for fear of what they would say. My family and friends would have thought

I had struck gold if I told them my earnings as a new hire. Comparatively speaking, it really was a lot. The giving spirit in me wanted to give to everyone back home even if I went broke, but I gave just a little and only when I thought it was necessary. I did not want them to think I was now so well-off that they could reach out to me for anything and I would give it to them. Yes, I was generous, but only to the point where I was not knowingly taken advantage of, especially since I needed to support my lifestyle, which I had taken up a few notches to reflect that I was now a US diplomat.

And then I moved to Manila, Philippines. Manila is fascinating and chaotic, but even with all its development, it seemed as if it couldn't accommodate all the people who crowded in and had to make home on sidewalks and on the sides of buildings. Even in the most rural part of Georgia, people might be poor, but they had a roof over their heads and something to eat. In Manila, children with runny noses and long tangled hair walked like zombies down busy, dangerous city streets with no shoes. Old cripples with no legs would pull themselves down the sidewalk on cardboard boxes or handcrafted skateboard-like mechanisms. Hundreds of old women would be bent over at the river washing clothes for hours. I'd peer out the window of the fancy American embassy motor-pool vehicle I was being driven in, aghast at the dismal poverty I saw. Lord, I was overwhelmed by it all. I wanted to give and help every one of them, but I knew I could not.

By the time I reached Africa, I hate to say it, but I had grown immune to seeing poverty all around me. Poverty, even though displayed differently than in other countries, was alive and well in Africa.

In comparing the Philippines with the first African country I lived in, I saw a large number of disfigured people and just as many with mental health issues. It was obvious that mental health programs were in great need, especially in the Philippines. In Africa, I was told that it was shameful for families to have a family member with "the condition," as they put it. They kept them at home, hidden away, but taken care of. In the Philippines, it appeared as if they exploited them. One too many times I was driving or in a car that would almost hit a child or elderly person who seemed like they were pushed out in front of the moving vehicle, forcing the vehicle to stop so hopefully someone in it would give them money. Thank goodness diplomats are given awareness briefings on the culture of the country so we would be prepared.

I didn't have a problem with giving to anyone who asked or who I thought would benefit from what I had to offer. Through the years, I'd give my housekeepers extra cash, clothing, and furniture, in addition to their salary, food, and transportation expenses. It wasn't required, but I fed my security guards, especially if they stayed beyond their normal shift because their relief did not show up on time. I'd drop coins in the glass of a man I passed daily on my commute to work, not giving a second thought to whether they were scamming or really in dire need. It could have been me in need, so I gave, and gave, and gave. If they scammed me, then they would have to explain why to God, not me.

Andrew was the same way when it came to giving. He'd scour the house for every cent of change and put it in his pocket. When our eyes would lock, he would say, "It is for the cripple man and the little boy on the street near the gas station, Momma."

One day while back home in Georgia on leave from the Philippines, he saw a nickel on the road. Just as he stepped out to get it, a car came around the corner and almost hit him. I quickly pulled him back and scolded him for almost getting injured or killed. With trembling, extended hands, he said, "Momma, look, it's a nickel. I am keeping this to give to the poor people back in the Philippines."

My heart fluttered, and tears formed in my eyes to discover that he had such a big heart at such a young age, just like his momma had. My parents give, I give, and now my dear child has the giving genes. "Chip off the old block do not fall far," as they say down South.

My peers at work always asked why I felt compelled to give all the time. Even my best friend Heather told me I had too much of a giving heart. If someone says *I like*, then *I give*, even if it's the clothes off my back. I've never needed to hoard my money or belongings. I do not need or desire much to live on, so giving down to my last dime—and I have done that, too—is easy for me. God always replenished what I needed and wanted (however, on his time), especially in my adulthood, so I never feel impoverished. Anxious and worried, yes, but never like I will die or go bankrupt. I believe in being thankful for what I have and figuring out ways to share it with others. Even if it's a piece of bread on my plate, I don't take it for granted. If I am not hungry enough to eat it, I wonder if someone else is hungry and wants it—just like Andrew and the nickel he saw in the street. He did not need it, but he still took it with the intent to give it to someone in need.

I can't fathom how some people are afraid to give or do not want to give. I have the opposite problem. Seeing so much poverty, how do I not give? Do you become numb to it? Turn a blind eye?

I understand that you must discern whether the need is truly there or not, but even if you give and get scammed, don't let it stop you. On the rare occasion I determine I should not give or if I don't have money or things to give, I give a kind word or a sincere smile, or I say a prayer in my heart for the person. *God, I can't give, but let this person find what they need somewhere else soon.* A simple prayer is sometimes better than giving something tangible because someone else may be in a position to give more.

As for me, I give whatever God lays upon my heart to share— money, prayer, clothes, food, etc. As someone of means, my responsibility is to give; the responsibility to receive is not mine. People shouldn't take advantage, but if they do, no matter. I've lived up to my end of the deal, and that's what matters.

It makes sense that I would be attracted to Shaka. He is a big-time giver, straight from the heart. When folks back in Africa would overwhelm us with their "wants," I would say to him with tears in my eyes, "Sweetheart, why don't they ask someone else sometimes?"

My giving husband would look at me and say, "Vella, it is my duty as a family member and citizen of the world to give when asked. But it is not my duty to ask why others in the family don't give. I give out of the goodness of my heart and not because of my obligation, so if I am asked and we have, please agree and let's give."

Eighteen years into our marriage, I still get overwhelmed and frustrated when his family asks for things that are "wants." Then,

I remember what Shaka said. He's right! Through his words, I finally realized some years back that the joy is indeed for the giver. I may give Shaka a hard time for a little while, but before long, I go to a nearby grocery store to Western Union the money to his family. I walk out of the store feeling truly good and joyful. Most of all, I feel like I am extra blessed when I call or text his family member to tell them the money has been wired.

"Thank you, my daughter, God bless you and Shaka," Momma or Papa Shaka would say.

"*Asante Sana*" I would reply.

Even though I balk at times, I take giving seriously because I believe God listens closely at my response when folks ask for things, but listens even closer at their response after they receive. When I give and someone says, "God bless you," I consider that a direct blessing through them from God to me. That blessing will keep me from getting shot or contracting a deadly disease one day, domestic or overseas. Don't get into the habit of giving and expecting a blessing soon after or for something you have asked God to bless you with. Your blessing will come when your heart is in the right place.

One of the most profound experiences I've had with this came when I was living in Sudan. We had to terminate a local staff member at the embassy. Consequently, many of his friends who also worked in the embassy weren't happy. As months passed, I would hear grumbling from time to time about his termination but thought nothing of it. One afternoon, one of my guards, who was from the southern part of Sudan where most of the black Sudanese came from, called and asked me to meet him in a local restaurant. I thought he wanted to discuss an Equal Employment Opportunity (EEO) issue since I was the volunteer EEO counselor for the embassy, or perhaps to ask how to get a better job in the embassy. On the contrary, I was shocked when he told me that the person who had been fired could be planning to retaliate against me.

"You need to be careful," he said. "Don't eat or drink anything given to you by a local. Don't go out on your own. If you have to, plan ahead, and I or one of the other black local guards will go with you if Mr. Shaka is not available."

I truly believe that it was God's blessing to send that guard to me with that message that possibly saved me from harm there in Sudan. I had always treated him and his fellow guards with respect, kindness, and generosity. I gave small gifts as tokens of my appreciation for their presence, asked about their children, sent clothes to their wives, and packed up food for them to take home to their families when I cooked a big meal. My generosity, in turn, protected me when I did not even know I was targeted.

The guards looked after me, especially after Shaka left the post of assignment to start his own Foreign Service career and I was alone to complete my assignment. On their free time, I would see a guard in the church or outside my church when I never noticed them there before. Even the drivers seemed more concerned and watchful. It was amazing. When I left Sudan for good, I was sitting in a comfortable airplane seat—not lying in a body bag in the airplane cargo hold. The blessing of generosity saves lives—it saved mine.

Another awesome blessing from giving I have experienced in my life occurred back home in Georgia. Some years back, I took my rental property off the market so that my 93-year-old Aunt Lucille could live there rent free after the family determined she was too old to live alone in her home in Florida. She decided to move back home to Georgia, where she was born and raised. Her spouse, Uncle Peter, had died many years before. I heard about her situation and offered her my house rent free to live forever. I thought nothing of it. It was sincere. The family could not believe it, but at the same time, they were relieved that she would be living in a nice comfortable home in a nice neighborhood. My mother said, "Bless you, Jane." Yes, another blessing for me.

Once Aunt Lucille settled in, she would take me aside each time I visited and say, "Jane, you do not know how grateful I am for you and Shaka allowing me to stay here and for free. God is gonna bless you, Shaka, and Andrew real big."

"Thank you, Aunt Lucille," I told her. "This is your home now. Enjoy it. We are glad we had it available for you."

Walking away, swinging her hips and legs from side to side, she'd say, "You just don't know, baby, you just don't know what you have done for me."

It hurt my heart when her health seemed to be on a downward spiral and it was best for her to be moved to a nursing home where she would have around-the-clock medical attention. Miraculously, her health improved so well over a period of a few years that Emma, my sister who made the personal commitment to see after Aunt Lucille in her old age, asked me if Aunt Lucille could return to the house.

"Of course," I said. "That's Aunt Lucille's house. Why ask such a silly question?"

This time around, Emma said she would be staying with Aunt Lucille since she was a bit more fragile than before when she lived alone. She made me promise to receive rent payment instead of her and Aunt Lucille staying there for free. I did not want to, and Shaka told me I was wrong to accept the money from family. Nevertheless, I humbly accepted the money for the rent because I saw it was important to my sister that I did. It was a timely blessing because we were struggling to rent the house, and since I was months away from retirement, the money came in handy to help Andrew pay his college tuition now that he had returned to his studies. I was most thankful for the joy of once again extending my house to Aunt Lucille so she could have a familiar place to live out the rest of her days, if it was God's will for her. She came back to the place she loved, surrounded by neighbors she had gotten to know when she lived there before. Friends and family were close enough for frequent visits. It felt like a blessing for me, and for what? For being generous, that's all!

For what I have accumulated through the years, it's not much, but it feels good to know that I have helped improve the quality of life for so many people, including an old widow—Aunt Lucille. It has taught me that being kind has no price tag. Generosity is never about money.

Gratefulness

Stop and breathe.
Now, be grateful!
I am overwhelmed yet grateful for it all—
the good, the bad, and everything in between.

My life changed in a remarkable way when I developed a heart of gratefulness. It's not enough to be thankful or to live up to expectations. It's not enough to be a giver if you don't give with a grateful heart. I know people who are accomplished and generous but conduct their lives as if they should have more and are entitled to it.

The start of being grateful expanded my heart and changed my disposition. I realized how much time and effort I had put into things that didn't really matter. Because all that matters, my friend, is loving and lifting the people we care about—even if you are a diplomat in the Foreign Service.

I recently read somewhere about keeping a gratefulness journal. Every day, write down something that makes you grateful. I decided to improvise by turning this last chapter into my own gratefulness journal that summarizes my life from the muddy roads of Holmestown to traveling all over the world and experiencing the unimaginable. Here goes:

I'm grateful to be alive and well today.

I'm grateful to be so alive that I am writing this book on how I left the muddy roads of Holmestown in pursuit of my dream.

I'm grateful for a mother who worked her fingers to the bone in the fields, around the house, and on temporary jobs to keep us fed and clothed when what my father brought home just wasn't enough. I wasn't the easiest child—I'm still not—but I love my mother and am so thankful for all she did for me. She was a loud big stick, never hesitating to challenge me and put me in my place. When I needed it most, she pushed me to become all that she knew I could be. I was her child; she knew me; she knew I had it in me. I thought she was being mean and insensitive when, in fact, she was being a caring mom amid rough times, raising me for success.

I'm grateful that I didn't get pregnant or do drugs when I was a teenager. It would have been so easy to go down those paths, but God and my parents' big stick kept me on another path that made me who I am today.

I'm grateful for a spirit of discernment. So many things that have happened to me were out of my control. I often wondered, *Why me?* But rather than have a pity party or feel victimized, I knew that things would eventually get better. I had enough sense not to do anything bad to an abusive husband. Even when I was overwhelmed with financial obligations and emotional burdens because of a bad marriage, I had enough sense not to neglect or give away my child.

I'm ever grateful that my son, Andrew, has a low-key personality, especially when he was younger. He and I had to be a team when we went abroad. If he hadn't listened to me through all those years, he (and I) could have ended up back in Holmestown—pitiful, yet again. I wouldn't have made it as a single black female in the Foreign Service if he weren't such a well-behaved child. He heard me when I told him he had to be a good boy so Mommy did not have to worry about him when she was working.

I'm grateful for the characteristics of my parents that gave me my unique personality. My mother was very conscious of her surroundings and paid attention to details in order to stay one step ahead of failure. She strived for and fought for us to have the best she could provide, and I got a little of that fight in me. My father, while not the best moral example at times due to his drinking, knew his shortcomings and often told me to learn from his mistakes—that spoke volumes to me.

I can't believe I'm writing this, but it's true: I'm grateful for the times I didn't get promoted when I and others thought I should have. I came in to the Foreign Service as a grade 09—the lowest level in the Foreign Service when I joined in 1989. It took a long time to climb the ladder to a grade 01, the highest one can reach before being promoted into the ranks of the Senior Foreign Service. It was a long and rough journey for me to get to grade 01, the goal I wanted to reach when I first joined the Foreign Service, and I could have fought my way to get there faster, but not at the expense of being angry and bitter. I wanted to get there in due time and on my own merits. I was smart enough. I was good enough. I was capable enough. And having to wait longer than I should have gave me a sensibleness about it all. It kept me humble and appreciative of all I accomplished, every step of the way.

I'm grateful to the work colleagues I've had over the years. I've had ambassadors and guards alike vouch for my character when

I needed it most. Colleagues who became friends have helped me through countless personal and professional situations. I've had subordinates who saw my lack of knowledge in some areas and picked up the slack for me, their boss, without boasting. I'm grateful for colleagues who allowed me to mentor them without saying I was patronizing.

I'm grateful to the Foreign Service for giving me the chance to travel and live internationally. Over 50 percent of my tenure was during a time absent the current level of terrorist activities, and as such, our lives were less hectic. I loved it. Andrew enjoyed it. My friends and family had fewer worries about us being abroad back then. The experience helps me accept others where they are. I became a lifelong learner. I think the Foreign Service life truly was the path that God showed me when I was only a kid dreaming long ago about what lay beyond the muddy roads of Holmestown.

I'm grateful for my siblings. They championed me throughout my journey. Without them, it would have been difficult from childhood to retirement!

My dear big brother Douglas, if you can hear me, I'm so grateful to you for giving me a wandering spirit. This brother took me the farthest away from Holmestown as a child—Tampa, Florida—so I would see a different way to live. The trips were short, but long enough for us to bond and further encourage me to want to travel. He encouraged me to be somebody other than a wife. If you can hear me, Douglas, thank you. I didn't become the runway model I told you I wanted to become, but I believe I did better than that—I became a model sister who helps other young females reach their potential. I love you.

I'm grateful for Loren, who supported me with a fighting spirit. She taught me how to keep folks from running over me. She stood up for me all those years long ago when I was being bullied on the bus, and she continued to stand up for me throughout my life until she passed away. Loren, if you can hear me up there in heaven, I love you and thank you for supporting me and loving my silly gifts and souvenirs I brought to you from my travels around the world. You used to wear those earrings and necklaces with style. It made me feel like a special little sister.

Sweet Rachel, I'm grateful for her unconditional love. It is all-encompassing, just like when I say, "I love you like a mom, friend, and a big sis!"

I'm grateful to Steven. I wouldn't have made it into the Foreign Service if it wasn't for his financial generosity to get me to the Oral Assessment. He gave me the money and said, "Break a leg, sis." Stern yet caring, he has shown me that even a serious person like him has a playful side. Being that Douglas did not grow up with us, Steven is my "big brother."

I'm grateful that Emma motivated me to be all that I could be. But I'm most grateful to her for not giving every time I asked. The disappointment turned to gratefulness when I became creative in resolving my own financial problems. I love you more than all the money you have, sis!

I'm grateful to Ronald. Being incarcerated can make a person hard, and he acts tough and hard but is a softy deep inside. He loves and trusts me. He was willing to allow me to adopt his only child and grandchild and take them around the world. He believes in me and tells me things in his unique philosophical way to make me a better person, and probably unbeknownst to him, he helped my son Andrew cope with the consequences of his indiscretions. It was painful to see Ronald incarcerated, and because of that pain, I made sure to be careful and intentional about how I raised Andrew. I know Andrew ended up with most of the same problems as his Uncle Ronald, but the foundation I laid for him that made him so resilient came from Ronald's experience. When young Andrew and I visited Ronald in jail, he would point his finger at Andrew and say, "Listen, Andrew, do not become like me. You better be good and listen to your mom." He did end up somewhat like Ronald, but it could have been worse in this day and age. I believe Andrew remembers those finger-pointing-in-his-face days. Live your life, brother, and forget about the past mistakes. Live for now and live for God! I love you, bro!

Ryan gave me the first opportunity to move away from home as a young adult. I am grateful that he asked me to come live with him and his Korean family upon graduating from college. I took him up on it and never looked back. Granted, I moved back to Georgia a few times to get my life together, but what he exposed me to was eye-opening and life changing, just like with Douglas when I was younger. I am grateful for him. We have a special bond that I hope will never be shaken by anyone. I love you, Mopao!

I'm grateful for you, Harold, who always makes me feel like a special little sister. In my early adulthood when we used to see each other, Harold would ask, "Are you being good, little sis?" Once I became successful, he started saying, "You have made something of yourself; I am proud of you, little sis." Thank you for making me a better wife to Shaka. I recall when we were getting into the limousine about to go to Daddy's funeral and I was fussing with Shaka about something small and insignificant, you said, "Baby sis, stop it. That is a man and your husband. He may be from another country, but you married him, so speak to him with respect." That resonated for years and calmed me down most of the time when I wanted to go ballistic on Shaka. Thanks, brother, you gave me the tools to save my marriage.

I'm grateful to Brittany. She took care of me when I was in college. I'll never forget going to the mailbox in Landrum Hall at Georgia Southern College and finding letters from her with money and notes inside: "Study hard, sis. This is just a little something from my small paycheck this month. Will send you more later." Thank you, sis—I needed the money and the encouragement. That is why when you used to ask for money, I never said no or asked for repayment. You deserved it and then some. Even though you think I was wrong for a lot of things, I really had no ill intention and seriously can't recall half of what you disclosed to me as being hurtful to you. Remember, I have grown up since my late 20s in different countries and cultures. Please take more time to understand me, and give me the opportunity to understand you—for both of us are quite different now. I am not too complex, but I am different. I loved being your best friend and need you back. I believe in miracles, so right now I am grateful to God for whatever blessing he has in store for us!

I'm grateful for my baby brother Eugene, "Junior," and his spiritual example. He isn't an ordained pastor but a strong spiritual leader for those close to him. He nurtured my faith through the years while living and working abroad by writing Bible scriptures on slips of notepaper and giving them to me to take back overseas. I thought it was so weird yet special. I still have some of those notes tucked away in my Bible.

I'm grateful to God for blessing me with the values I have shared in this book. I consider them small compasses for survival. I was blessed to know to take God and my compasses with me around the world just like Reverend Arthur Stevens told me in church when he found out I would be working and living abroad. "Take the Lord with you," he said. A forgiving heart and an unwavering faith are very precious compasses.

I'm grateful for the prayerfulness of my mother. She didn't hide her love of God from us, and she openly called upon him in need or in joy. She would walk slowly through the backyards of the old and new house sites waiting for my daddy to come home (with whatever he had remaining of his paycheck), humming spiritual songs and planning how she would make ends meet. When I rode with her in the car to my college graduation, she sat in the back seat singing, "Thank you." When each brother returned home from the military, she would sing and praise their return. When I came home after the embassy bombing in Tanzania, she sang "Amazing Grace" all the way home from the airport.

After Hurricane Matthew passed through the eastern part of the United States in 2015 and none of my family was harmed, my mother sang a medley of gratefulness songs in the hotel in South Carolina where we went for safety.

I am grateful for a lifelong friend, Heather. Being overseas, it helps to have people and places back home to think about and long for. It helps you get through the long days and nights abroad. Even through the times we grew apart, the thought of returning home and bumping into her made me yearn to return home. Now that we are both a little older and wiser, I am grateful we salvaged our friendship the few times it was on the rocks.

And finally, for Shaka, who forever changed my perception of family and life in general and made me stronger than I thought I could ever be, I will be forever grateful. Shaka made me understand the true meaning of family and the extraordinary role they play in our lives. He was, and continues to be, a tremendous support in helping me through everything with Andrew. He encouraged me to talk openly with my family about my problems instead of hiding them and acting like my life was great. He said: "Vella, if you tell them first, you will save them the agony of talking to you about it, not give them the pleasure of talking behind your back and smiling in your face, and save you the embarrassment of them telling you about it." He said, "Tell them and be free, Vella." It works. He showed me the difference between giving out of love versus the feeling of giving out of pity. He made me think differently about what had happened and still is happening in my life. In his deep African voice, he says, "Vella, it is the path God has laid, and it can't be changed." I thank God for waiting until that perfect time to bring Shaka into our family. We all love Shaka.

For everything that has come before—the happiness, the pain, the love, the hatred, the joy, the disappointment, the sickness, the sorrow, the weddings, the divorces, the birth, the career, the promotions, the friendships, the crises, and the retirement—I am grateful for it all.

51006035R00124

Made in the USA
Columbia, SC
15 February 2019